MURDER & CRIME

LINCOLN

MURDER & CRIME

LINCOLN

DOUGLAS WYNN

The History Press

Frontispiece: A horse fair in the High Street, Lincoln, 1890s. (From the Illustrations Index, by courtesy of the Lincolnshire County Council – LCL 2492)

First published 2011

The History Press
The Mill, Brimscombe Port
Stroud, Gloucestershire, GL5 2QG
www.thehistorypress.co.uk

British Library Cataloguing in Publication Data.
A catalogue record for this book is available from the British Library.

ISBN 978 07524 5921 9

Typesetting and origination by The History Press
Printed in Great Britain

CONTENTS

Acknowledgements   7

Introduction   8

1. Killer Conman   12
   John George Haigh, 1948-9

2. A Lethal Obsession   22
   Christopher Barker, 1893

3. Murder Will Out   30
   Thomas Cash, 1606

4. A Tragedy of Love   36
   Sarah Clarke, 1885

5. Manic Murder   42
   William Drant, 1876

6. A Drowning in the Fossdyke   49
   Hannah Wright, 1895

7. 'I never thought it would come to this'   56
   Joseph Bowser, 1897

8. A Fatal Affray   62
   Joseph Bones, 1866

9. Shots in the Night   67
   William Clarke, 1877

10. A Kind of Justice?   74
    John Carrott, 1858

11. Borstal Boy   81
    Kenneth Strickson, 1948

12. A Murderous Pair   85
    Henry Carey and William Picket, 1859

13. No Provocation   91
    Leonard Holmes, 1945

Bibliography   95

ACKNOWLEDGEMENTS

I should like to thank the staff at the Lincoln Central Library, the Grimsby Central Library, the Boston Central Library and the Louth Library for their kind and helpful assistance. My grateful thanks are also due to my friend Richard D'Arcy for his help with research and pictures. Also to Teresa Goreck for her help with the Nottingham stories. Thanks also to Ged Payne for images from The Illustrations Index and Nick Tomlinson for images from 'Picture The Past'. I should particularly like to thank Nicola Guy and Matilda Richards at The History Press, for their help during the writing of this book. And, as always, to Rosemary, for without her this book would have never have been written.

INTRODUCTION

A Short History of Lincoln

The Romans landed in England in AD 43 and when the Ninth Legion subsequently marched up from London they followed the line of a limestone ridge which runs down the western side of what is now Lincolnshire. There is a gap in this ridge where the River Witham widened into a lake, now called the Brayford Pool, and turned at right angles to flow through the gap and continue south east to the coast at Boston. This was an ideal place to build a fort, and the Roman's constructed one on the northern summit of the gap. They also built the road called Ermine Street, which ran from London to Lincoln and then on to York, and the Fosse Way, which linked Exeter with Lincoln and marked the western limit of the Roman occupation. The fort was called Lindum from the Celtic word *lindo*, meaning a pool. The Roman forces eventually moved north to York and the fort was converted into a town for the settlement of retired soldiers. It was then called *Lindum Colonia*, which later became Lincoln.

When the last Roman soldiers left the country in about 407, the town had grown and spread down the hill to the river and beyond. The Romans had also deepened the Witham and constructed the Fossdyke canal linking the Witham with the Trent. But in a short while the town was abandoned and the Roman buildings fell into ruins. When the Danes came in the ninth century they established areas called boroughs centred on the old Roman towns of Lincoln, Leicester, Derby Nottingham and Stamford. Later the Stamford borough became joined with the Lincoln and thus Lincolnshire was established. The Danish language also gave rise to many place names: 'Gata' meant street and gives the names Clasketgate and Danesgate, and in Lincolnshire there are 217 place names ending in 'by', from the Danish word for village.

William the Conqueror won the battle of Hastings in 1066 and by 1068 had built a wooden castle in Lincoln (which later, in the twelfth century, was converted to stone). It had two fortified mounts, or towers (called mottes). On the south side are the Lucy Tower, which was the original keep, and what is now called the Observatory Tower. The large bailey or courtyard was enclosed by earthen banks surmounted by stone walls. The bailey originally contained the Shire Hall where the sheriff held his court, quarters for the constable in charge of the castle and his soldiers, and a prison. The originals have all disappeared but there remains to this day the Assize Court and the remnants of the subsequent prisons. Indeed, the sturdy walls we see these days were preserved when the castle ceased to have any military use, because of a prison within it.

By the time of the Norman Conquest Lincoln had become an important city of around 6,000 people. London only had 18,000 at the same time. In 1072, the bishop of Dorchester, Remigius, moved to Lincoln and began building the cathedral. It was finished in 1092, but almost a hundred years later the central part was damaged by an earthquake. It was rebuilt, however, but the central tower collapsed in 1237. Again rebuilding took place; the new tower had a spire on the top, and was completed in 1311.

Lincoln also became involved in the battles between King Stephen and Matilda and was sacked twice, once in 1141 and then in 1216. But the prosperity of the town continued to increase, based largely upon wool, which was woven and dyed in the city and transported along the Witham. In 1291, Lincoln was made a 'staple' which allowed it to export wool. But as time went on the city suffered competition from other counties and countries overseas, and in 1369 the wool staple was withdrawn and moved to Boston.

This caused the city to go into a decline which lasted for almost 400 years and the population dropped to under 2,500. In 1548 the great spire of the cathedral, which at 525ft (160m) had made it the tallest building in the world, collapsed and had to be rebuilt. Although the Wars of the Roses largely passed Lincoln by, the city was involved in the Civil War between Cromwell and King Charles I. The city changed hands several times, but in the final months of the war in 1648 the royalists attacked, but were driven off by a relieving force of roundheads.

After the civil war, Lincoln became a small market town and in 1700 had a population of around 4,000. But it retained some of its functions from medieval times. The bishop ran the diocese from the cathedral and assizes were held in the court in the castle in spring and late summer. By the middle of the century there was an improvement in communications. The Fossdyke was deepened, enabling wool and grain to be shipped to the Trent and the north. A new courthouse was built in the castle courtyard in 1776, but the building began to slowly subside and was replaced with one which subsequently opened in 1826. This is the one that remains today.

From about the 1850s Lincoln changed from being a market town to being an industrial centre. Engineering works moved into the town, notably Clayton and Shuttleworth, who made steam engines and farm implements, and brickmaking and brewing industries were begun. From a population of about 7,000 in 1801, Lincoln rose to over 50,000 inhabitants by 1900. The population grew more slowly in the twentieth century but the industry remained largely based on engineering. During the First World War, the first tanks were made in Lincoln, from an idea put forward by the chief engineer of Fosters Engineering Works, William Triton. Many aircraft were built there as well. By the end of the twentieth century heavy industry in Lincoln had been replaced by service industries and tourism. The population of the city stands in 2011 at 87,000.

Crime and Punishment in Lincoln
Cobb Hall, the small tower situated at the north-east corner of the castle, was constructed in the thirteenth century and had dungeons in its base where prisoners could be housed.

They were often chained to the walls and kept in darkness. These were mainly prisoners of war. The county gaol, built in the castle bailey in late Tudor and early Stuart times, was intended for crimes committed by Lincolnshire people living outside the city. Lincoln citizens were housed in a prison at the Guildhall in the Stonebow, the old southern gate of the city.

In 1781, Britain lost her colonies in America after the War of Independence, and transportation to those colonies ceased. This caused something of a crisis and triggered the building of new and larger jails. The new jail in the castle was built in 1775 and extended in 1847. Nevertheless, transportation still continued, this time to the new colonies in Australia. Transportation was mostly for petty crimes, such as stealing small amounts or poaching. But felons convicted of more serious crimes which carried the death penalty, such as stealing livestock and horses, burglary, coining and murder, might be reprieved and be sentenced to transportation instead. Usually the sentence handed down by the courts was for seven years, fourteen years or life.

The first fleet of convict ships left for Australia in 1787 carrying 548 men and 188 female convicts and arriving in Port Jackson, later known as Sydney Harbour, some eight months later. A second fleet sailed in 1789, and between 1788 and 1867 150,000 convicts were transported from Britain. Of the transported convicts, a total of 1,200 came from Lincolnshire. In the early years conditions on the ships were appalling. Four men, each wearing leg irons, had to share a space 6ft by 7ft. It was impossible to stand upright and the space below the deck was difficult to ventilate; the smell must have been dreadful. In the tropics the heat was insupportable. A quarter of the convicts on the second fleet died before they reached their destination.

Hanging at Lincoln originally took place outside the castle walls, near the north-west corner of the castle. There is a pub on the site called the Strugglers Arms and executions took place outside the pub until the late eighteenth century. The gallows was simply a crossbeam supported by two posts. The condemned man was driven up in a cart, a noose placed round his neck and – after prayers were said and the prisoner addressed a few words to the crowd – the cart was driven away. The condemned man swung until he slowly strangled to death, unless his friends pulled on his legs to hasten his death or the hangman could be bribed to do it.

Public executions were the rule, and to make the Lincoln hangings more public it was decided to conduct them on the roof of Cobb Hall so that they could be seen from the streets around the castle. From 1817 all executions were carried out there, usually on a market day to ensure a bigger audience. Thousands would attend, and they became eventually like riotous public holidays. The spectacle revolted a great many people, however, Charles Dickens being one, and they campaigned for the end of public executions. This came about in 1868; thereafter executions took place in the courtyard of the castle at a spot near the court house. Although a new prison was opened on Greetwell Road in June 1872, no executions were carried out there until 1883.

An alternative to the strangling method of hanging was proposed by William Marwood, a Horncastle shoemaker, in 1872. He became official executioner on the retirement of William Calcraft in 1874. Marwood's more humane method was to estimate the length of drop necessary to break the neck of the prisoner, when the knot of the rope was placed under the left ear, causing a quick death. His method was taken up by all the subsequent hangmen until the death penalty was finally abolished by Parliament in 1969. The last hanging in Lincoln took place in 1961.

Although this book is called *Murder & Crime: Lincoln*, I have used the city only as a base, showing its exciting and dramatic history, and selecting some cases from its streets. But to add variety I have spread the net wider and chosen violent and terrible episodes from around Lincolnshire and even some from outside the county – though all the hangings described in this book, except for one, took place in Lincoln.

Douglas Wynn, 2011

One

KILLER CONMAN

John George Haigh, 1948-9

'Why Mrs Durand-Deacon, you do look smart today,' said Mrs Constance Lane.

'Well thank you,' said Mrs Deacon, pulling her Persian lamb coat around her more closely with one hand while the other flaunted a smart red plastic handbag. They had met on the stairs of the hotel, Mrs Durand-Deacon coming down and Mrs Lane going up. The Onslow Court Hotel was a very genteel establishment in Queens's Gate, South Kensington, mostly occupied by elderly but wealthy ladies. It was the afternoon of 18 February 1949, just after lunch.

'And where are you off to then?' persisted Mrs Lane, a trifle coquettishly.

Mrs Durand-Deacon went faintly pink, but she recovered herself quickly. She was, after all, sixty-nine years old, the widow of a colonel in the Gloucestershire Regiment, and she had lived in the establishment since 1942. 'Well,' she said conspiratorially, 'I'm going to meet that very nice young man who has the table next to mine in the dining room.'

'Oh are you?' This time the words were drawn out in a most provocative manner.

'Of course the meeting is entirely about business,' replied Mrs Durand-Deacon. She was having none of these insinuations, even though Mrs Lane was her best friend in the hotel. 'He has a business down in Horsham or Crawley, I think. He's some kind of inventor, you know. And I've had this idea for some time of paper fingernails that can be stuck on to ordinary fingernails and would prevent wear and look very nice. And he's going to see about producing them for me. We're going down to his workshop this afternoon.'

The gentleman concerned had been living at the Onslow Hotel since 1944. He was thirty-nine years old, a small, well-dressed man with thick, carefully brushed dark hair and a small moustache. His manner, polite, attentive and obliging, had endeared him to most of the ladies in the hotel – though not, it is true, to the lady manager. His name was John George Haigh, and he was about to murder Mrs Durand-Deacon and dissolve her body in acid.

Haigh was born on 24 July 1909 at 22 King's Road, Stamford. His father, John Robert Haigh, was a skilled electrical engineer and a Station Superintendent for the Urban Electric Supply Co. Ltd during the building of the works in Wharf Road, Stamford.

King's Road, Stamford, where Haigh was born.

Both John Robert Haigh and his wife Emily were staunch members of the Plymouth Brethren sect and their religious views dominated their only son's childhood. Books, newspapers and the radio were banned in the household. Young George, as they called their son, was not allowed to play with other children and his parents never mixed with other families who were not Plymouth Brethren. Prayers were said every day, as were readings from the Bible – and by all accounts George's father was a strict disciplinarian.

The family did not stay long in Stamford. In the December of that year, George's father lost his job as the electrics works was completed and the company laid off the staff. But almost immediately he obtained another position with the Lofthouse Colliery Co. near Wakefield and began working at the Outwood Colliery. The family moved to the village of Outwood on the outskirts of Wakefield, and it was there that young George went to school. All his teachers said that he was a bright, intelligent lad, always smartly turned out and always polite and obedient. But he was extremely lazy, virtually ignoring the subjects he did not like. He found, however, that he could lie easily and was rarely found out. And he also discovered that he had a talent for forgery, which started off as a game at school, but later developed until he eventually became one of the most accomplished forgers in the country. He also had a talent for music. At the age of nine he won a choral scholarship to the Wakefield Grammar School and, in spite of his parents' religious beliefs, sang in the choir at Wakefield Cathedral. He was a gifted pianist and in later years often entertained his friends with recitals.

John George Haigh left the Grammar School in 1926 when he was seventeen, without taking his school certificate (the equivalent in 2011 of GCSEs) and went to work in a garage. His employer Mr W. Gillott afterwards said, 'He was lazy. He often came to work an hour late. But he had great charm and in spite of his failings I had to like him.' But he didn't keep him long and Haigh flitted then from job to job. But he was ambitious, and by the time he was twenty-one had started his own agency, selling advertising, insurance on commission and dealing in house sales. He is said to be the first to sell advertising space on electric signs. He turned out to be brilliant at figures and he learned quickly about conveyancing and real estate. But the money didn't come in fast enough for him. He craved the high life: expensive cars, good clothes and all the luxuries money can buy.

By this time he had moved to Leeds and he started a hire-purchase business selling cars. Except that there were no cars. He forged contracts with hire-purchase firms for fictitious buyers and fictitious cars and pocketed the money from the hire-purchase firms. But instead of using some of the money to pay off some of the premiums, and thus stave off discovery, he kept the cash, and the fraud was soon discovered.

In the meantime he had got married. She was Miss Beatrice Hamer, a waitress in a Leeds restaurant, a very pretty woman and a former photographic model. Her parents were vaudeville artists, working mostly in the north of England. Haigh was twenty-four years old and Beatrice twenty-one, and they were married in July 1934 in Bridlington. They also had their honeymoon there. The marriage lasted just four months. In the November, Haigh was tried at the Leeds Assizes for conspiring to defraud, aiding and abetting the forgery of a document and obtaining money by false pretences. He was sentenced to fifteen months. During his imprisonment, a daughter was born to his wife. But Haigh never claimed paternity, and as far as is known his wife never visited him in prison. She stayed for a while with his parents but left after a short time. The baby, Pauline, was adopted and Beatrice never saw Haigh again.

While Haigh was in prison he learned that the Plymouth Brethren had expelled him, and this caused him acute distress. On his release he approached a friend of his father, full of remorse and pleading that he would be a reformed character. The man, who was a solicitor, took pity on him and set him up in the dry-cleaning business. Once again he quickly learned the business, but once again the lure of quick and easy money was too much for him. He left and set himself up as a solicitor, stealing a name he found in the Law List. He gravitated to people likely to be interested in stocks and shares, and offered shares from the estate of a recently deceased client at a specially reduced price. But he asked those interested in buying leave a deposit of 25 per cent of the cost. Of course there was no estate, and no shares. But his powers of forgery were such that many people were completely fooled and the money began to roll in. When people began asking for their share certificates he simply moved to another town and set himself up under another name he had taken from the Law List. But he slipped up when he got to Guildford. He misspelled the name on his letter head (he left the 'd' out). The police were soon on to him, and on 24 November 1937 at the Surrey Assizes he received four years' penal servitude.

He served most of his sentence in Dartmoor, but by August 1940 he was out on licence. He came to London and took lodgings in St James Street. Life in London at the time was chaotic. There was constant night-time bombing, and the blackouts maintained to deter the bombers gave ample opportunity for thievery and muggings in the darkness that prevailed. But there was plenty of money about, as forces personnel on leave with money in their pockets gravitated to the pubs and night clubs. Black-market traders abounded, so-called 'spivs' operated on street corners – and everything, including rationed food and petrol, could be had at a price. It wasn't difficult either for a crafty operator like Haigh to avoid National Service, and he got a job as a fire-watcher.

But Haigh couldn't resist the lure of looting from bombed-out properties, and in June 1941 he was sentenced at the London Sessions to twenty months' hard labour for stealing

High Street, Stamford.

five bunks, kitchen equipment worth £17 10s, and sixty yards of curtaining material and a refrigerator. Part of his sentence he actually served in Lincoln Prison, in the tinsmith's shop – where sulphuric acid was used and stored. The story goes that he persuaded other prisoners who worked outside in the gardens to bring him in field mice and he used these to experiment with, dissolving the bodies in sulphuric acid.

One of the great money-making devices of 1930s and 1940s London was the pin-ball machine. At the time gambling was illegal in England, except on racecourses, but pin-ball machines were considered to require some skill and therefore were not considered games of chance. Every public house had one or more, and arcades of them sprang up on every High Street. One of the men who made fortunes from the machines during the 1930s was a William McSwan. He and his son, Donald, owed many of the machines and made so much money that they were able to buy property in Raynes Park and Beckenham. For a brief period Haigh had worked for them as a secretary/chauffeur but had subsequently moved on to other projects.

When Haigh came out of prison he met the McSwan family again. William and his wife were now retired and had left the running of the business to Donald. Haigh decided to take a leaf out of their book and go into the pin-table business himself and he began by repairing pin-ball machines. He rented a basement flat at 79 Gloucester Road to use as a workshop, but he used to meet Donald fairly regularly in The Goat public house in Kensington. One day in 1944, over a few beers, Donald confessed that he was worried about being called up.

'You mean you don't want to be called up?' asked Haigh.

Donald nodded.

'Nothing easier, old chap. Go on the trot. Get lost. Go away. If you are not at home you can't receive call-up papers, can you?'

'That's all very well. But where can I go? I'd need my ration book and identification card. The authorities would catch up with me quite easily.'

'Yes, I see that, Donald. Tell you what. I'll give it some thought. There are ways of slipping under the wire, you know. I did it. I evaded call-up. Let me see if I can make some arrangements.'

Whether the idea occurred to Haigh there and then or whether it subsequently came to him we do not know. But Donald McSwan was a valuable quarry. He had a very good income from the operation of the pin-ball machines; he had money in the bank and his family had a lot of valuable property. If Haigh could get his hands on it he would a very rich man indeed.

On 9 September 1944, Haigh invited Donald to 79 Gloucester Road, ostensibly to discuss how Haigh could arrange for him to go under cover. When the young man had his back turned, Haigh picked up the leg of a pin-table machine and battered him to death with it. Then he had to dispose of the body. He found a water butt on a disused bomb site and carried it in a cart to the basement at Gloucester Road. He put the body in it. He had some acid he used for pickling and he poured it in by means of a bucket. The process, however, took longer than he expected, and at one stage he had to resort to cutting up the body with a cleaver and a large mincer he bought from Gamages. But after seventy-four hours the body was completely dissolved, and he poured the resulting solution and sludge down the drain in the basement. Then he went round to Donald's parents' house and told them their son had gone to Scotland to avoid the call-up. A week later they received a letter from Glasgow purportedly from their son saying that he was fit and well and not to worry about him. The forgery was so good that Mr and Mrs McSwan suspected nothing. Haigh continued to send forged letters from Donald asking the McSwans to send him money – through Haigh, of course, as he was the only man Donald said he could trust to send it. But when they heard that their son was giving Haigh instructions to sell the amusement arcades, they grew anxious, and William demanded from Haigh Donald's address in Scotland so he could go and talk him out of the foolish idea.

So Haigh invited the two to Gloucester Road, and they disappeared as well. Haigh then impersonated Donald McSwan himself and forged his signature, thus obtaining a power of attorney. By this means he was able to sell the properties in Raynes Park and Beckenham and eventually to liquidate everything that the McSwan family owed. It is estimated that he made over £4,000 altogether. It seems that the family was not missed. In fact, their disappearance only came to light when Haigh finally admitted to their murder.

Haigh was now in the money. He moved into the Onslow Court Hotel, bought a new and very expensive car and threw his money about as if there was no tomorrow. By August 1947, however, he was £25 5s 2d in the red. He was behind with his rent at the hotel and owed money to several hire-purchase companies. Then he saw an advertisement in a newspaper for the sale of a house in Ladbroke Square. He went to see the house and met the owners, the Hendersons. Dr Archibald Henderson was fifty years of age and a rich man; his first wife died in 1937 and left him £20,000. He no longer practiced medicine but

Wharf Road, Stamford, seen from the bridge over the River Welland.

lived a life of luxury, staying in the best hotels and throwing expensive parties. His second wife, Rosalie, had formerly been the wife of a German inventor. She was dark, attractive and wore expensive jewellery, but she wasn't initially impressed with Haigh. After his visit she wrote to her brother: 'Of the scores of stupid people I've met, I've just been introduced to the greatest of them all. I offered him 22 Ladbroke Square, lock, stock and barrel for £7,750, and he said, "That's too cheap, but if you will accept ten thousand, it's a deal".'

Haigh had no intention of buying the house, however, and he never did. After prevaricating for several weeks, the Hendersons got fed up with him and sold the house to someone else. But surprisingly Haigh managed to keep on good terms with them – and even to ingratiate himself with them. He ran errands for them, bought tickets for the theatre, played the piano for them and took them on trips in his expensive motor car. By this time he had given up the Gloucester Road basement, although he was still staying at the Onslow Court Hotel. He had managed to get himself made the London representative of a firm concerned with light engineering in Crawley, called Hurstlea Products. The firm had its main premises in West Street, but also had a storeroom in Giles Yard, Leopold Street. This was a small two-storey brick building and Haigh had somehow got hold of the key. Unbeknown to the firm, Haigh ordered carboys of sulphuric acid to be delivered to the storeroom together with two 40-gallon drums.

At this time, February 1948, Haigh was £237 overdrawn at the Westminster Bank. He owed £400 to a money lender and he was, as usual, in arrears with his rent at the Onslow Court Hotel. The Hendersons were staying at the Metropole Hotel in Brighton with their red setter. Haigh drove down there on the 15th in his Lagonda and invited Archie Henderson to go with him to see his research laboratory in Crawley. He took the man to the Leopold Road store room and shot him in the back of the head with his own revolver, which he had previously stolen from the Henderson home. Then he went back to

Brighton and told Rosalie that her husband had been taken ill and needed her and offered to drive her to him. He took her to the storeroom, killed her there and disposed of the bodies in the 40-gallon drums with the acid.

The next day he went to the Metropole Hotel and paid the Hendersons' bill. He produced a letter of authority, apparently signed by Archie, and took the dog for a walk on the beach while he had the hotel staff pack up the Hendersons' luggage and load it into his car. Then he drove off. He immediately sold Mrs Henderson's jewellery for cash – all except for a very nice, almost new red plastic handbag which he sold to Mrs Durand-Deacon for £10. He sold Archie's car and by means of forged deeds disposed of the Hendersons' house in Dawes Road, Fulham. The dog he put in kennels and asked the owner to find a good home for her. By forging letters from Mrs Henderson to her brother he gave him the news that the Hendersons had gone to Scotland and then that they had decided to immigrate to South Africa. But Mrs Henderson's brother was used to her telephoning him frequently and he became worried when he received no more calls. He received a number of letters, which were such good forgeries that he was convinced they really came from her, but he was still uneasy. He contacted Haigh, who told him that Archie might be in some trouble and that might be why they were so difficult to contact. The brother remained only partially convinced. At one time he considered going to the police, but then he didn't. Not until it was too late to save anyone else, anyway.

It was just a year later, on 19 February 1949, when Mrs Durand-Deacon disappeared. She did not come down to breakfast the next morning and because she was such a creature of orderly habits, Mrs Lane was disturbed. Haigh came over to her table.

'Do you know anything about Mrs Durand-Deacon?' he asked. 'Is she ill?'

Mrs Lane looked up at him. 'I'm sure I don't know, Mr Haigh.'

'Do you know where she is?'

Lincoln Prison, where Haigh was incarcerated in 1941.

Mrs Lane had never liked Haigh. She thought that he was far too smarmy and he seemed to hang round the elderly ladies far too much for her taste. 'Well, Mr Haigh, I'm surprised you asking that. I understood from Mrs Durand-Deacon, whom I met on the stairs yesterday afternoon, that you were going to take her to Horsham, or was it Crawley, I'm never quite sure these days what people tell me.'

This was not what Haigh wanted to hear. He hadn't realised that the two ladies had spoken on the stairs the day before. He must have wished he hadn't raised the subject with Mrs Lane. But being Haigh, he rose to the occasion. 'That's quite true,' he said smoothly. 'But I wasn't quite ready. I hadn't had my lunch then. And Mrs Durand-Deacon said she wanted to go to the Army & Navy Stores, so she asked me to pick her up there. But though I waited for over an hour there she never turned up.'

Mrs Lane was very concerned about her friend. She asked the chambermaid to look into Mrs Durand-Deacon's room, and the girl reported that the bed had not been slept in. She consulted the hotel manageress, Miss Robbie, who told her that Mrs Durand-Deacon always told her in advance if she was going to be away for even a short time. The next morning at breakfast Mrs Lane said to Haigh: 'I'm very worried that some harm may have come to my friend. I'm going to report her disappearance at the Chelsea police station. Since you could confirm the arrangement she made with you, perhaps you would like to come too?'

'Of course I will. I'll do anything I can to help.'

They were interviewed by Sergeant Alexandra Lambourne. There were few female police officers in those days and they were often consigned to disappearance cases, since those were not considered to be of a criminal nature. But Sgt Lambourne had the traditional police feeling that there was something wrong somewhere. And she had a deep suspicion about John Haigh. She wrote all this in her report and it was noticed by Detective Inspector Webb. He went round to the Onslow Court Hotel himself and talked to the manageress, Miss Robbie, to Mrs Constance Lane and finally to Haigh. Haigh told the inspector that he was in partnership with a man called Jones who ran the Hurstlea Products firm in Crawley, and that he did experimental work at the storehouse in Leopold Road. Webb had the same feeling about Haigh that Sgt Lambourne had, and when he got back to the Chelsea police station he consulted the criminal records to see if anything was 'known' about John Haigh. Indeed it was.

Webb immediately contacted his superiors, who decided that there were grounds for extending the investigation. A description of the missing woman was circulated to the national press, together with a photograph and particulars of her jewellery and the clothing she had been wearing when she disappeared. This soon brought the information that Mrs Durand-Deacon's Persian lamb coat had been sold in Sussex; some of her jewellery, it seemed, had been disposed of in London, and the description of the man who sold the items matched that of John Haigh. Two officers went down to Crawley, and in the storeroom in Leopold Road they came across ration books and clothing coupons relating to people called McSwan and Henderson. They also found what looked like a splash of blood on one of the inside walls. Webb was instructed to bring in Haigh for interview.

He went immediately to the Onslow Court Hotel, but Haigh was not there. In the hallway he found two packed suitcases with Haigh's name on them. Haigh had apparently gone to fetch his car. Webb waited and when his man appeared asked him if he would come to the station for another interview.

'Well,' said Haigh. 'I was just on my way to see my solicitor. Can't it wait until I've seen him?'

'I'm afraid not, sir.'

At the interview Haigh was confronted with the evidence of the ration books and clothing coupons and the sale of the fur coat and jewellery. He admitted being in possession of the ration books and selling the coat and jewellery, but claimed that the owners had gone abroad and asked him to dispose of their possessions.

'I believe you've murdered these people,' challenged Webb.

'You can't prove a murder without a body,' smiled Haigh.

'Oh yes you can. There was a recent case where a man pushed a woman through the porthole of a ship on the high seas. Her body was never found, but he was convicted of murder. And]there was a case in Ireland when a son murdered his mother and pushed her body into the sea. It too was never found, but he was convicted of murder. And you must have heard of the 'Bluebeard' case in France; Landru, who killed probably eleven people, though none of the bodies were ever found.' Webb smiled. 'He was guillotined,' he remarked pleasantly.

John Haigh sat and considered this for some time. It was obvious that he was considering different options. An insanity plea might save him from the gallows. Suddenly he said, 'What are the chances of getting out of Broadmoor?'

'I can't possibly discuss that sort of thing with you.' But Webb knew that it was only a matter of time now before Haigh confessed. And he was right. A short time later Haigh made a full confession. But it was such an incredible confession that Inspector Webb had never heard anything like it in his whole life.

John George Haigh. (Police photograph taken at Horsham police station, 1949.)

Haigh began by admitting taking Mrs Durand-Deacon to Crawley in his car; while she was examining some paper for use as fingernails he shot her in the back of the head. He then went out to his car to collect a drinking glass and proceeded to drink some of the lady's blood. It was the same with the others, the McSwans and the Hendersons. In every case, he claimed that after killing them he had drunk their blood.

The case caused a sensation in the national press. Headlines like 'Acid Murders in Cellar' appeared in many national dailies. But when Haigh was charged with murder on Wednesday 2 March the case became *sub judice*, which meant that nothing prejudicial to the accused could be published. However, the *Daily Mirror* decided to publish the story of the vampire murderer's confession without actually naming him. But Haigh's legal advisers took the case to court and the judge considered it a most serious contempt of court. Sylvester Bolam, who was editor of the *Daily Mirror*, was sent to prison for three months and the newspaper fined £10,000.

Dr Keith Simpson, the noted forensic pathologist, went to Crawley and made an extensive examination of the storehouse and the ground outside it where the sludge from the acid bath had been poured. He found two gall stones, which Mrs Durand-Deacon was known to suffer from, eighteen pieces of eroded bone and an upper and a lower denture, which were afterwards confirmed by her dentist as having come from Mrs Durand-Deacon. So Haigh was wrong when he thought he had completely destroyed the body.

He went on trial for the murder of Mrs Durand-Deacon only, at Lewes Assizes, because the murder had taken place in Surrey, on 18 July 1949. The judge was eighty-two-year-old Mr Justice Travers Humphries, soon to retire, and the prosecution was led by the Attorney General, Sir Hartley Shawcross. The trial was the sensation of the age. Hollywood stars came over from America to attend it, and the newspapers of the day published virtually nothing else. But it only lasted two days. The prosecution produced the forensic evidence, Haigh's confession and a succession of witnesses to support the evidence. Sir David Maxwell Fyfe, the defence counsel, could do little except produce Dr Henry Yellowlees, a consultant at St Thomas's Hospital in London, who tried to claim that Haigh did not know what he was doing. His evidence was totally destroyed by Sir Hartley Shawcross in cross examination and he was made to admit that within the law Haigh was not insane. Haigh did not go into the witness box himself. The jury took only a quarter of an hour to convict him of murder.

On Monday 10 August, John George Haigh met his final acquaintance in the shape of the executioner, Albert Pierrepoint, at Wandsworth Prison in London. But perhaps the final word should go to Haigh's mother, who, on her death bed, said, 'We used to despise people in the village because we thought we were God's elect. But we were not.'

Two

A LETHAL OBSESSION
Christopher Barker, 1893

In the 1890s, Danesgate, Lincoln, was a quiet thoroughfare. Most of it looked on to the St Andrews cemetery to the east (in the area which is now occupied by the Usher Gallery), and it ran down, as today, to Clasketgate. Some of the houses were quite substantial with three storeys, including an attic, but they were terraced and had small backyards. In 1890, at No. 47, there lived three people, Christopher Barker, his wife and a young schoolmaster who was their lodger. He was twenty-five-year-old Crosha James Creasey and he was a schoolmaster at the Wesleyan School. He was slightly crippled in that he walked with a stick. Christopher Barker was fifty-six and as far as is known they had all lived together happily until Mrs Barker died in December 1890. Then Barker became very depressed.

Barker had a reputation for being eccentric. He had worked as a joiner for many years at the Ruston Proctor and Co. Woodworks and his workmates there considered him rather peculiar. He often talked about suicide and asked his companions whether they wouldn't like to go to Heaven. And he had once told a workmate that if he did commit suicide it would be by shooting as he considered this more heroic. Latterly he had been working at Cannon and Co, and the workers there remarked that he had become very dejected and moody since his wife died and had seemed to lose all sociability.

Christopher Barker engaged a young girl to look after the house and cook them meals when his wife died. She was the niece of his late wife, a Miss Wilkinson, who was nineteen, and whose parents lived in Grimsby. She lived in and had her own room. During May of the following year young Creasey went on holiday for a week, and when he returned Miss Wilkinson said she would like to speak with him privately and ask his advice. She told him that when he had been away her employer had come into her bedroom one night as she was preparing to go to bed and had tried to behave improperly towards her. She was very much upset by this and she asked Creasey what she should do. He advised her to leave. After some hesitation, she finally told Barker that she was going to leave; naturally, he wanted to know why. Bit by bit the truth, the came out – and Barker was furious. Creasey took the young girl's part and a row developed between the two men. This culminated in Creasey leaving as well. But the enmity between the two men festered in Barker's mind and it was to have long-term consequences.

Whitewashed cottages in Danesgate, Lincoln, 1900s. (From the Illustrations Index, by courtesy of Lincolnshire County Council – LCL9671)

Creasey only moved next door to lodge with a Mrs Lucy Wilkinson, who was no relation to Barker's niece. Mrs Wilkinson was a strong, determined woman who had the reputation locally as being a person who minded her own business and never talked about her domestic affairs outside the home. She had been married three times. She had a daughter with her first husband and the daughter was now married and lived in Reepham. Her second husband was called Phillips, and with him she had a son and a daughter. The son, Charles Phillips, still lived with his mother at 45 Danesgate, together with one of her grandsons called Partridge. Charles Phillips worked at Robey's Foundry. Phillips himself had died sixteen years ago and Lucy married again, this time to Wilkinson; he too had died, and she was now a widow. It was rumoured in the street that she was a woman who liked being married and that she was setting her cap at Creasey. This seems a little unlikely since there must have been a considerable disparity in their ages, but it is true to say that she did keep a motherly eye on the young man, who was not that much older than her son Charles.

The enmity between the two men became an obsession for Barker. He took to writing Creasey abusive letters and if he saw him outside, shouting and swearing at him. He even attacked him once in the street and the two had to be separated by neighbours. Young Charles Phillips advised him to 'have him up' for it. But Creasey, who must have been a quiet and inoffensive fellow, only replied, 'Leave him alone. Let it be quiet and it will turn out all right.' Barker also accused Creasey of having an affair with Mrs Wilkinson.

It all came to a head one Monday afternoon in May 1893. Creasey had just left the house to go to work when Mrs Wilkinson heard Barker shouting at him outside the window. She heard Creasey say, 'I've never done you any harm.' Then she herself went outside, only to be met with jeers from Barker. 'You needn't bring the missus out to talk to me!' Then Barker turned to Mrs Wilkinson directly. 'You don't want to associate with him. He's a nasty, dirty, whoring scamp!'

But Mrs Wilkinson would not be put off by Barker. 'You should feel ashamed of yourself for saying that about him, after he has been such a good friend to you, especially when your wife died.'

View of Danesgate in 2011

Barker looked away. 'He was a good friend to me once,' he muttered in a low voice.

Since the attentions of Barker were now turned away from him, Creasey had slipped away and made his way to his school. But Mrs Wilkinson was not going to let Barker get away with saying things like that. 'You want to be careful what you say, because I can make you prove your words.' But this set him off again. 'I know what I'm talking about,' he snapped.

By this time, however, the noise of the argument had attracted a crowd, mostly of young children on their way to school, and anything that promised more excitement than a boring afternoon at school was an obvious attraction. But Mrs Wilkinson was so embarrassed to hear her lodger being called names in front of a lot of schoolchildren that she gave up the argument and went indoors.

At about six o'clock that same evening Mrs Wilkinson heard some raised voices in the back yard; going out she saw her son Charles talking to Barker over the garden fence. He was accusing the older man of being rude to his mother.

'No I wasn't,' said Barker, banging his hand down on the wooden fence.

'Oh yes you were!' chimed in Mrs Wilkinson.

'You're a liar!' shouted Barker.

'You can take that back!' shouted Charles in return and made as if to climb over the fence to get at the older man. But Barker backed away. 'If I was rude to her I don't remember saying anything like that,' he mumbled.

'Well, what about apologising to my mother?'

'All right,' he said ungraciously.

But if mother and son thought that was the end of the argument, they were mistaken. For after a few moments of silence – in which Barker seemed to be working himself up again – he burst out with all his previous accusations, calling Mrs Wilkinson a liar and repeating his accusations about the young schoolmaster. 'If you'll fetch him out here I'll thrash him,' he shouted.

'Well he isn't here,' replied Mrs Wilkinson. 'He's at school tonight.' But she could see the futility of arguing with the distraught older man and, grabbing her son by the arm, she pushed Charles inside the house and followed him in.

The next afternoon, Tuesday, she was at the front door of her house seeing her little grandson off to school when Barker appeared in the street again. He leered at her. 'Have you got anything to say to me today?'

She pretended she hadn't heard him and carried on saying goodbye to her grandson. But Barker repeated his question.

'No,' snapped Mrs Wilkinson. 'I don't want to talk to a man like you.'

But Barker wouldn't be denied. He carried on calling Creasey a dirty, whoring scamp and said that he would 'do for him'. She wouldn't have him for long and she would have to 'wail for him like an old cow'. And just to complete the tirade, he called her a strumpet and a bad woman.

It was the last straw as far as Mrs Lucy Wilkinson was concerned. Nobody was going to call her names in public and get away with it, and when Creasey came home that afternoon she persuaded him to go with her to see a solicitor. They saw a Mr Williams in town and took out two summonses against Barker. One was for abusive language against Mrs Wilkinson and the other was for threats against Creasey. Sergeant Cole of the Lincoln City Police served the summonses on Christopher Barker the following afternoon. Barker at first seemed surprised to get them, but then he muttered that he would see about them the next morning.

He came round to No. 45 at about nine o'clock the same night and knocked on the front door. It was opened by Mrs Wilkinson's son.

'Is Mr Creasey there?'

'No, he isn't.'

Barker shuffled his feet for a moment. 'Will you ask your mother to come and speak to me?' Charles fetched his mother, and when she had appeared Barker said, 'Don't you think this is a very paltry affair?'

'No, I don't. My character has been taken away in public by you and I want some recompense.'

Barker was silent for some time, chewing his lip. 'Can't we settle this thing between ourselves, without going to law?'

'No, we can't.' And she shut the door in his face. She locked the front door and put out the lights. But soon afterwards there came another knock at the front door. Lucy warned her son not to answer it. Then there was a knock at the back door. She locked this as well and didn't answer the knock. There was a period of silence and then there was another knock at the back. This time she said, 'Who's there?' But there came no reply. 'I'll not open the door unless you tell me who's there.' But again there was no reply and the knocking then stopped. All at No. 45 went to bed. But about one o'clock in the morning Mrs Wilkinson heard someone moving about in the back yard. She could hear someone walking up and down and then they began kicking at the back door. This went on for an hour or so but then the kicking stopped.

A view of Clasketgate.

The next morning, Thursday, Mrs Lucy Wilkinson was out in the back yard cleaning boots when Barker came out into his yard. She could see him over the garden fence. His face was red and he was plainly still very angry. He started on again about the summonses, eventually saying, 'Who's going to pay for them?' Lucy ignored him at first but then he said, 'Can't we make it all up?'

'No, we can't. I've told you before you've taken my character away.'

Barker said no more for a while, but plainly he was fuming inside. Eventually he burst out, 'I want to talk to Creasey.'

'He's still in bed. You'll have to wait until he gets up.'

'I'm not messing about with you. I'm going to speak to him now.'

'No, you're not!'

But by this time the older man had climbed over the backyard fence. Lucy made a rush for the back door, which was open, but Barker was faster and caught up with her as her hand was on the door. He reached his arm around her neck, pulled out a revolver from his pocket, pressed the barrel against her ear, and fired. Mrs Wilkinson fell unconscious on the ground and Barker stepped over her and rushed upstairs.

All this had been witnessed by another neighbour, a Mrs Sarah Kelham, who lived nearby and had been out in her back yard as well. She heard another shot coming from No. 45, and then she saw Christopher Barker appear at the back door and calmly walk out, climb over the fence and disappear into his own house. Mrs Kelham climbed over the fences to reach Lucy Wilkinson, who was now unconscious on the ground with blood pouring from her ear. Then Mrs Kelham went into the house and up the stairs to Creasey's bedroom, which was at the front. But she couldn't get the door open. Something seemed to be jammed up behind it. She rushed downstairs and out of the front door looking for a policeman. She saw a young boy passing and told him to go for a policeman. Then she went back to look after her neighbour.

PC Abbott was soon contacted and he sent a man to fetch a doctor. Dr Mounsey, who had a house and surgery on Steep Hill, quickly arrived at No. 45 Danesgate. In the back yard he found two women bathing Mrs Wilkinson's wound and with their help, and that of PC Abbott, they got the injured woman to bed. Then the doctor and policeman went to Creasey's room. They forced the door open and found Creasey behind the door lying on the floor. He had bullet wound over the left eye and he was dead. He had apparently been in the act of shaving when he was shot by Barker. Back went the doctor to Mrs Wilkinson. He examined her and found that she was alive but going in and out of consciousness. He ordered that she should be taken to the County Hospital.

By this time the Chief Constable of the City of Lincoln, Mr William Marshall, had arrived with Sergeant Cole and PC Bugg. He made a brief inspection of No. 45 and then went next door to No. 47, accompanied by PC Bugg and PC Abbott. The back door was locked but when he knocked Barker appeared at a downstairs window brandishing a revolver.

Barker was the first to speak. 'You'll not come here. If you do, you see this,' he waved the revolver at them. 'Well, this is what I'll do.' And he put the barrel of the revolver in his mouth.

'Don't do that,' said the Chief Constable. 'Open the door and let me in and we'll talk.'

'I shan't. If you come any nearer I'll do it!'

'What do you want to shoot yourself for?'

'What's the use of living to be hanged? Is the woman dead?' William Marshall shook his head. 'Is the man?'

Looking up Steep Hill, Lincoln, 1900s. (From the Illustrations Index, by courtesy of Lincolnshire county Council – LCL 18514)

But the Chief Constable made no answer. Instead he said, 'You open the door and I'll tell you all about it.'

The policeman kept the conversation going with Barker for a further ten minutes or so. In the meantime Sgt Cole and PC Bugg, who had remained behind at No. 45, had found a ladder. They took it around to the front of No. 47 and climbed up. Luckily for them there was an upstairs window which was not properly shut and they managed to push it open. They climbed into the bedroom as quietly as they could and crept down the stairs. Silently they eased into the back room where they saw Barker, with the gun in his hand, still talking to the Chief Constable through the window. Sergeant Cole rushed him and, gripping the arm holding the gun, forced it up so that Barker could not use the pistol on himself. While this was going on PC Bugg unlocked the back door, letting in the Chief Constable, and between them they managed to secure the furiously struggling man and put the cuffs on him. While the two PCs took Barker away to be charged with murder, Marshall and Sgt Cole remained behind to search the premises. They found a box containing cartridges and a number of letters resembling a will, in which Barker wrote that he wished certain objects to be given to certain people. In one, addressed to another joiner, he wrote: 'Please make me a coffin just like my dear wife. Law is master of me but justice I have. They are dishonest, but they will suffer.'

The inquest opened on Friday night at the Marquis of Granby Inn and after hearing witnesses the jury brought in a verdict of wilful murder against Christopher Barker. On the same day, Barker was brought before the magistrates at the Lincoln City Police Court and committed for trial at the assizes. The Lincoln Summer Assizes opened on 10 July,

The Assize Court, Lincoln.

before Mr Justice Vaughan Williams and a number of magistrates, aldermen and councillors of the City of Lincoln, and before a grand jury at the Sessions House. This used to be at the bottom of Lindum Road, just to the west of where De Montfort University now stands. After the grand jury had brought in a true bill against Barker the court adjourned to the castle, where the trial was held in the Assize Court building.

The prosecution was in the hands of Mr Buzzard QC and Mr Gilmour, and Christopher Barker was defended by Mr Stanger and Mr White. Their only defence was to try and prove insanity, and to this end they brought a number of eminent medical men to give their opinions. These included Dr Lindsey, Medical Superintendent of the Derby County Lunatic Asylum, who considered that the prisoner was definitely of unsound mind. The defence also called witnesses to show that Barker's paternal aunt, Louisa Frankland, was decidedly peculiar. She would get up in the night and shout out that somebody was in her room and trying to murder her, and she would lock her bedroom door and put wedges under the door 'to keep them out'.

But all this went for nothing. Two medical witnesses brought by the prosecution gave it as their opinion that Barker was not insane and the jury required only twenty-five minutes' deliberation to bring in a verdict of guilty of murder. Christopher Barker was sentenced to death. But perhaps the efforts of the defence did bear some fruit, because days before he was due to hang he was reprieved and sentenced to life imprisonment.

Mrs Lucy Wilkinson survived to give evidence at the trial, a large bandage wrapped round her head, but beyond that nothing more is known of her.

Three

MURDER WILL OUT

Thomas Cash, 1606

It was the Elizabethan era. Christopher Marlowe was making his way in London, probably as a Government spy, but also writing *Dr Faustus*, among other plays. William Shakespeare was also in London as part of a group of actors, and he was beginning to write his plays and falling under the influence of Marlowe. Abroad, the Newfoundland colony was founded in the so-called New World and, in 1584, Walter Raleigh, who later became Sir Walter Raleigh, discovered Virginia and made several attempts to found a colony there. Nearer home, Sir Francis Drake was instrumental in organising the defeat of the Spanish Armada in 1588. But in quiet rural Lincolnshire, a murder occurred which reverberates down the years to today.

In those days there were no local newspapers to report on local happenings, since few people could actually read. There were schools, but these were mainly for those who could afford the fees. There were parish constables, but organised police forces were not established for another 250 years. There were courts, but often a murderer could escape justice by fleeing the area, sometimes going abroad, or by changing his name; provided he was not recognised he might remain free for a long time.

Holton le Moor village sign.

High Street, Holton le Moor.

But there were occasions where a murder might be reported and written about. It might be because the case was an unusually gruesome one, or it might be that the case could be told as a horrible example of what might happen if a person gave way to his or her baser passions. Religion was an important part of most people's lives in the sixteenth century and religious writings often used murder cases to illustrate the pernicious influence of the Devil.

Such was the case in Lincolnshire, in the hamlet of Holton le Moor. Today it is a pretty village just off the main road from Grimsby to Market Rasen and some twenty miles north of Lincoln. In 1581 it was a much larger settlement with a number of trades and tradesmen in the village. One of these was a young man called Thomas Cash, who was a tailor. He was married to Ellen, who had been born Ellen Greame and came from wealthy parents who lived in Yorkshire. So it was quite likely that she came with a substantial dowry and this would have helped to make Thomas Cash – rather fittingly – relatively well off.

But it seems that the relationship was not a happy one. They only had one child in an age when large families were very common and it is reported that Ellen believed that this was due to the fact that Thomas spent too much of his time with a Mrs Newton, who was a neighbour. She believed that he 'had the use of this woman', as it was quaintly put at the time. Whether this was true or not, it is a fact that Mrs Cash suffered ill health and was confined to her bed for a lot of the time. However, medical science at the time was of the most rudimentary kind. There were few doctors and they mostly practiced in big towns. In villages, most people would consult a wise woman, and be doctored with various herbs and traditional remedies. But Ellen Cash's illness went on for some seven years and she proved to be a difficult and fractious patient.

The Cash family had a servant called Anne Pottes and she noticed and commented upon her mistresses' ailment. She also had another reason for speaking about it. She could see that Thomas was irritated by his wife's condition and reasoned that if his wife should die she might have a chance of becoming the next Mrs Cash. On one occasion she said to him, 'Master, Mrs Cash is becoming every day more troublesome to herself and to you sir. It might be better for her and for others if she were to leave this world.'

In those days serious illnesses were rarely cured and death for one reason or another was very common. It would be relatively easy to end the life of a sickly person and, provided there were no obvious signs of violence, it would be taken as a death from natural causes. It seems that this idea began to take hold of Thomas Cash's imagination and he discussed it with his servant, pointing out that they had suffered these seven long years with having to look after their difficult patient. And if she was willing to keep the secret he would think of a way of secretly disposing of his wife.

Anne Pottes thought this was too good an opportunity to miss. She readily agreed, feeling that if she was involved in such a nefarious plot she would have a hold on her master and he would be sure to marry her afterwards. And so there came a time in 1581 when Ellen felt a little better and decided to get up from her bed and come and sit by the fire. Thomas decided that this was time to act. Ellen had asked him to get her something and he walked behind her, apparently to get her what she asked for, and grabbed her by the throat, forcing her head back with his right hand while, with his left, he clamped a cloth over mouth and nostrils so that she could not breathe. She struggled only briefly, being weak from the illness, and soon subsided.

Thomas called Anne to him. 'I've done the deed. This is the end of our long and continued trouble. We'll wait for a few minutes until we see that she actually is dead, that she's not breathing anymore. Then I want you to rush out and shout that your mistress has had a seizure and get as many of the neighbours as you can to come in and help. Suggest they bring some brandy or something to try and revive her and save her life. And if you can, pretend that you are desolated by her death. Can you do that?'

Anne promised that she could, and was as good as her word. She dashed out, screaming that her poor mistress was dying, and the neighbours soon followed bearing spirits to try and revive the stricken woman. They were met with Thomas weeping in a corner and bewailing his bad fortune in having lost his wonderful wife. They commiserated with him while they struggled to bring Ellen back, but it was no use: she was dead. While some stayed to comfort Thomas, others set about arranging the funeral, for this would be an occasion when the whole village would turn out. There was no autopsy, and no death

North Owersby.

The church at Middle Rasen.

certificate was required in those days. Death was so common in the village that it was taken as a fact of life. Ellen Cash was buried the next day in the local churchyard amid a large crowd of mourners.

Soon after the funeral, Anne was anxious that she and Thomas should make plans for their wedding. But Thomas pointed out that it would undoubtedly cast suspicion on the pair if they were seen to be too much together and he advised Anne to be patient and for them to carry on much as they had been before. She reluctantly agreed. But the next startling turn of events came a few weeks later, when Mrs Newton's husband died suddenly. Again it was the occasion for another funeral and it seemed only natural to many in the village that the recently bereaved Thomas should comfort the also newly bereaved Mrs Newton.

But Anne found the association not to her taste. She was afraid that he would go back to his previous relationship with the neighbour. She tackled him about it, but Thomas told her that she was being overly suspicious and that he was just being neighbourly towards the woman. But Anne would have none of it. She was convinced there was more to it. And she was becoming angry. 'Don't forget, my master,' she cried, 'what you have done with your wife. It would go ill with you if I were to tell what I know. And if you persist in this business with Mrs Newton I may be forced to speak out.'

Thomas's face went red but he controlled himself. Nevertheless, when he did speak it was with a certain menace. 'Listen to me, my girl. You are involved in that business as much as I.'

'What? Why, I had nothing to do with it. It was you that killed the poor woman.'

Thomas's face twisted into a sneer. 'And who do you think is going to believe that? What do you think people will say when they remember that it was you who rushed out of the house and shouted for people to come and help your poor mistress? Do you think they will believe you had nothing to do with her death, when you said nothing about the evil deed at the time?'

Anne looked shocked. 'Well I didn't have anything to do with it. I only did what you told me to.'

Thomas shook his head as if he was trying to explain things to a particularly stupid person. 'What about those conversations we had, where we talked about ending her life? And you agreed to keep the secret if I should go ahead and end it. No, listen!' he said, as Anne tried to expostulate. 'If you now say that you know I killed my wife but you didn't say anything at the time, in law, you will be judged to part of the conspiracy, even if you did not take part in the deed. And being part of the conspiracy will get you hanged just as if you did the deed yourself!'

Anne's face registered the conflicting emotions which ran through her head. She was a country woman with little knowledge of the law and she had an unpleasant feeling that what Thomas said was right and that she would be hanged as well as him should she speak out. But there was nothing that she could do. She simply had to accept the situation. And the inevitable happened. The widow Newton was a much better prospect for marriage for Thomas than Anne Pottes, since the widow had property of her own, and within six months of the death of Ellen Cash, Thomas and Mrs Newton were wed. But although the marriage undoubtedly upset Anne Pottes, it also upset many in the village who felt that the marriage had been too hasty. It also raised suspicions in people's minds that perhaps Thomas's wife's death had not been from natural causes after all. But although suspicions were rife in the village there was little that could be done.

The old bridge at Middle Rasen.

Thomas Cash, however, felt that the close proximity of his servant in the village would prove too much of a temptation for her to speak out and he gave her money and persuaded her to leave the village, and it is known that she went to London. It has been reported that Thomas himself began to have attacks of conscience and couldn't bear to stay for long in the room where he had killed his wife. On the other hand, it might well have been pressure from the villagers that unsettled him. But after a couple of years he and his new wife left Holton le Moor and went to live in the village of Long Oarsbie (now called North Owersby) which is few miles south of Holton le Moor.

There it seemed that his conscience did not trouble him so much, and he stayed there in apparent tranquillity for some eighteen years. His second wife died in 1595 after fourteen years of marriage. And after a year and a half of being a widower he married again, this time to a Jennet Mowse, with whom he had two children. They moved again, this time further south to Middle Rasen, in 1599.

Little is known of what happened to Anne Pottes except that, near the end of her life, she came to live in the parish of St Leonard's, Shoreditch, in London. She was ill and feared that she would soon die. But she still had the fearful secret on her conscience and was afraid that should she died without confessing her sins she would not go to heaven. She called the minister of the parish to her and poured out her story. But the minister warned her that it was a sin to accuse someone of such a terrible crime as murder. When Anne replied that it was the truth, and seemed so sorrowful and penitent, the minister was disposed to believe her. He prayed for her and read her some of the appropriate scriptures and assured her of the remission of her sins. And she died peacefully soon after.

Because the confession was not made in church and therefore was to his mind unofficial, the minister felt that he was able to tell the appropriate authorities about it. Sir Richard Hamsotes, the High Sherriff of Lincolnshire, was in London at the time and he was informed of the confession. He immediately signed an order for the arrest of the murderer. Cash was taken to Lincoln Castle and there examined by Sir William Wray. He made a full confession saying that he was relieved from something which had been on his conscience for twenty-five years. He was tried on 20 November 1606 and executed soon after.

Four

A TRAGEDY OF LOVE

Sarah Clarke, 1885

Adolphus Hawkins was a porter on the Midland Railway. On a bright sunny morning in June 1885, he watched the 11.33 train from Grimsby puffing into the Midland station at Lincoln. When the train had clanked to a halt and the doors swung open, and passengers began to disembark, he saw a young woman step down from a carriage. She had two small children with her. One was a baby, whom she carried on one arm, and the other was a two year old, who clutched her hand. She turned back to look into the train and a man inside pulled out a trunk for her and placed it on the platform before tipping his hat and getting back in the train. She smiled her thanks and looked around for a porter. Adolphus hurried up and placed the trunk on his barrow and at a word from the woman wheeled it over to the left luggage, where she checked it in and duly received a ticket. She turned to Adolphus and gave him a bright smile and then left the station, leaving Adolphus to wonder how he had missed out on a tip. The woman's name was Sarah Clarke. She was twenty-eight and the reason she didn't give Adolphus a tip was that she was practically destitute. Her story is one of the most amazing in the annals of love and murder.

Some ten years before, young Sarah had been living with her parents in Lincoln. Their lodger was a smart young man called Joseph Clarke. He was very much attracted to Sarah, and she to him, and they soon became lovers. But the inevitable happened and she became pregnant. In those days this was a serious social offence and likely to bring disgrace upon Sarah and her parents. Her parents therefore insisted that the couple get married. Reluctantly, they did. They decided to make the best of it and with the help of Sarah's parents rented a house on Steep Hill. Joseph, who was only a labouring man, found difficulty in finding a job, but eventually he found a position with a firm in Gainsborough. He went into lodgings in the town and returned home at weekends. But the arrangement apparently didn't suit Sarah and one day at his lodgings Joseph received a letter from Sarah telling him that she was leaving him. He raced back to Lincoln but found the house on Steep Hill empty and Sarah and the baby gone.

Eight months later, he received a letter from his wife in Bradford pleading to be forgiven and asking him to take her back. In the 1880s it was difficult for women to leave their husbands.

Looking down Steep Hill, Lincoln, 1900s. (From the Illustrations Index, by courtesy of Lincolnshire County Council – LCL 18307)

The money in the family was controlled by the man. If they did have money of their own it was still considered to be the property of their husbands. Employment opportunities were also very restricted for women, especially if they had young children. Joseph agreed to take Sarah back and they appeared to live harmoniously together – and another child, the second one, was born. But the reconciliation did not last, and Sarah went off again. Two months later she came back again and a third child was born.

This time they decided to make a fresh start in another town and moved to Hull. But Joseph's wage was small and to help with the finances Sarah suggested that they take in a lodger. Joseph agreed, and soon a young man called George Taylor moved in with them. But the usual story took place, and Sarah went off with the lodger. Joseph now had three children to look after, so he decided he would be better off moving back to Lincoln. He did so, but eighteen months later who should arrive at his house but Sarah, bringing with her the child she had had with George Taylor. Incredibly, Joseph took them both in, so there were now two adults and four children living in the house (though it must be said that large families were the norm in those days).

The wandering Sarah had itchy feet and before long she had gone back to George Taylor. He was now living in Gravesend and Sarah joined him there. It turned out, however, that Taylor was the one this time with no desire to stay, and after six months or so he left Sarah – but he also left her pregnant. This put her in a very difficult position: she now had two children to look after and her only resource was the poor law. But Sarah had a better idea. She wrote again to Joseph saying she was deeply sorry for what she had done and that if he took her back she would never leave him again. And the tender-hearted Joseph agreed once more to have her back.

But here the story departs from the old familiar pattern. Joseph had by this time moved to another house in Lincoln, in Shepherd's Buildings, Little Bargate. He employed the daughter of a neighbour to look after the children when he was out at work. And after a short period the young woman, Emma Truelove, moved in with him. This had the effect of stiffening Joseph's resolve and he wrote to Sarah telling her not to come as he had changed his mind. Sarah received this second letter on Tuesday 23 June. But to her way of thinking she had no alternative but to come back and she set out on her journey the following day. The quickest way would have been by train to London and then on to Lincoln. But this was the most expensive route. The much cheaper, but much more roundabout one, was to get a coastal steamer from Gravesend to Hull, then across on the ferry to New Holland and on to Grimsby where she could get a train to Lincoln.

Sarah arrived at Lincoln on Thursday 25 June. There was of course no Joseph to meet her, but this did not deter Sarah. She had to see him to try and persuade him to take her back, but also because she was desperately short of money. She knew where he worked, the premises of Burtt & Roper, timber merchants, in Portland Street, and she assumed he would be at work that afternoon. Portland Street was only just across the road from the Midland station and Sarah, grasping her children, dashed across the busy High Street avoiding the trams that ran down the middle. When she had reached Portland Street she approached a young boy. She asked him if he would go into the premises and ask for Mr Clarke and tell him that his wife was outside and wanted to speak to him. The young boy did so and eventually a not very pleased Joseph came out to speak with her. We don't know what was actually said, but we

Little Bargate, Lincoln.

do know that Joseph was now determined not to have Sarah back. And he told her that he wanted nothing more to do with her. And although Sarah cajoled and pleaded, Joseph, for once, was firm, and he went back inside leaving Sarah to fret on the pavement.

Apart from her disappointment, Sarah had two fractious children to cope with. They were hungry and tired. The long journey had taken its toll on all of them. Sarah trailed the children up and down the High Street for a long time until she finally settled on a café which advertised rooms to let. She took the two children inside and the proprietor, Mrs Mary Doncaster, took pity on her and gave her a cup of tea and prepared some gruel for the children. Sarah told Mrs Doncaster that she was expecting a letter from her husband in Bradford, with some money for her, and she was on her way to meet him in Bradford. On this promise, Mrs Doncaster allowed her a room. Sarah put the children to bed and then said she was going up herself as she had a headache.

The next morning, Friday, Sarah came down at nine o'clock with the children washed and dressed and they all had breakfast in the café. Afterwards, Sarah asked Mrs Doncaster if she would look after the children for her as she had to go out and see if the money her husband had promised to send her had arrived. She came back later that morning looking extremely depressed and said that the letter had not arrived for her. In reality, it seems quite possible that she had made another attempt to see Joseph and he had refused to meet her. Mrs Doncaster reported later that Sarah seemed depressed that afternoon and was very tearful. When Mrs Doncaster asked what the matter was, Sarah said that she still had a sick headache. Later that afternoon she asked Mrs Doncaster if she could send someone to the left luggage office at the Midland station to reclaim her trunk and she gave Mrs Doncaster the ticket. That lady sent one of her sons and he brought back the heavy trunk and took it up to Sarah's room. Sarah opened it and took out some clothes. Then, after again asking Mrs Doncaster to look after her children, she went out, carrying the clothes. She returned after a period without the clothes, but with some money with which she paid Mrs Doncaster for her board and lodgings. After another meal she again went up to bed early, saying that she still had her sick headache.

The next morning at about nine o'clock Mrs Doncaster expected Sarah and the children to come down, but they didn't. She went up and knocked on the door, but received no answer. The door was locked. Since she had other boarders to see to she went away, and it was only much later in the morning that she returned to Sarah's room and again knocked on the door. There was no reply from Sarah, but Mrs Doncaster thought that she could hear a child crying. Thinking that something must be wrong, she instructed her servant girl to get the ladder from the outhouse, climb up and look in the window. The girl quickly came down again saying that she thought something terrible had happened.

Mrs Doncaster sent her for the police, and Sgt Cole, who had been on duty in the High Street, soon arrived. He too went up the ladder, and managed to push up the window and climb inside the room. Sgt Cole was the same policeman who eight years later, in 1893, again climbed up a ladder to get into a house, this time the house of Christopher Barker. In 1885 the room he entered was quiet. All three in the bed appeared insensible. Sarah seemed cold and the two children had laboured breathing. He sent at once for Dr Harrison. When the sergeant attempted to turn Sarah she was immediately sick. But she seemed to regain consciousness. 'I wish you'd let me die,' she mumbled. 'It's all through him. I've taken laudanum and given the children some.'

When the doctor arrived he took the children into another room, but there was little he could do for them and both died later that day. Sgt Cole found a dress on the bed and in a pocket discovered three small bottles. Two were labelled poison, but the third was not. There was also a tumbler and a spoon on a table near the bed. Further police enquiries showed that Sarah had pawned clothes for 2s 9d. She had then purchased three separate 'three pennyworths' of laudanum from three separate shops in Lincoln that Friday afternoon. Sarah later confessed that around four o'clock on Saturday morning she had given the two children a spoonful each of the laudanum and taken the rest herself.

Portland Street in Lincoln

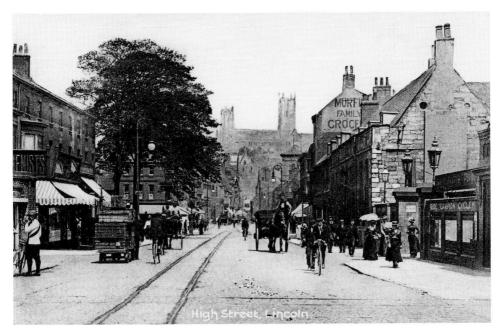

High Street, Lincoln, 1900s. (From the Illustrations Index, by courtesy of Lincolnshire County Council – LCL 18269)

Although laudanum, which is a solution of morphine, was known to be a poison, until the early 1900s it could still be purchased without the formality of signing the poisons register provided the solution was less than 1 per cent. And mostly the solutions sold were 0.7 per cent. It was also quite common in Victorian times to administer small doses of laudanum to children to quieten them down.

A post-mortem was performed on the bodies of the two children on the following Monday and the inquest was held in the Hare and Hounds public house at seven o'clock the same evening. Subsequent analysis determined that the two children had died of morphine poisoning, and the result of the eventual inquest was a verdict of wilful murder against Sarah Clarke.

She went on trial for murder at the Lincoln Assizes on 24 July 1885. The prosecution was in the hands of Mr Mills and Mr Kennedy and she was defended by Mr Etherington Smith. He asserted that she could have accidentally given the two children overdoses of the poison when she merely wanted to keep them quiet while she herself wanted to commit suicide. But the prosecution asserted that four o'clock in the morning was an unreasonable time to give children medicine. The jury took a lenient view of the situation, seeing the circumstances under which Sarah was placed, and brought in a verdict of manslaughter after only eight minutes' deliberation. The judge was lenient too, sentencing her to eighteen months' hard labour.

Five

MANIC MURDER

William Drant, 1876

The little village of Hemingby lies four miles north of Horncastle and some eighteen miles from Lincoln. It nestles under the Wolds along a small stream which shortly joins the River Bain which itself runs down to Horncastle. Hemingby has a church (St Margaret's) and one pub, the Coach and Horses. In 1876 it was a much larger village with a population of around 420 people, and there was, in addition to the church, a Wesleyan chapel. There was also a Free School for children of the parish with a schoolmaster and a school mistress. It had been founded by Jane Lady Dymoke in 1772 and endowed by her with a yearly salary for the teachers and a provision for clothing six children and apprenticing some of them to agricultural trades. There were also four almshouses endowed by the same lady.

Cottages in Hemingby village.

Then, as now, it was largely a farming community. But there were a number of shops in the village, which also boasted a miller and baker, several carpenters and boot and shoe makers. There were two blacksmiths and a wheelwright, who was also a shopkeeper and a maker of agricultural machinery. His name was Thomas Bett Gell and he was fifty-three years old. He only had one eye, the other being damaged in an accident at work, but he was at the time of this story serving as a part-time parish constable.

Being a parish constable was not a popular job. They were appointed by local ratepayers for a year at a time and were unpaid. They had no proper training, yet were expected to deal with drunken youths, complaints about noise and pubs abusing the gaming laws. They had to supervise prisoners, put them in stocks or the lock-up and then take them before the magistrates. Even when a professional police force was formed in Lincolnshire in 1857, parish constables were still kept on and formed a valuable part of it.

One of the blacksmiths in the village was a William Drant. He was thirty-eight years old in 1876. He had been born in the village and had been apprenticed to his uncle, who had a blacksmith's business; he took over the business when his uncle retired. He was a short man but powerfully built with strong arms and shoulders (as befits a blacksmith). He also suffered from epilepsy, and had frequent fits. Not much was known about the condition in those days: in fact, many people did not recognise it as a medical condition at all. But there were some who did. Henry Maudsley was a leading psychiatrist of the time, and he wrote:

Epileptics appear to be sane enough and even amiable, industrious and well-behaved before their fits, but these unfortunate persons become immediately after them most violent and destructive beings for a time. And when they come to themselves they are utterly unconscious of what they have done in their state of alienation.

Contemporary view of Hemingby village, with St Margaret's church in the background and the Coach and Horses on the right.

William Drant had a couple of fits on Tuesday 10 October of that year and the following day four or five seizures. He was living with his mother, Mrs Jane Drant, at the time, since his wife had left him. He had already served a prison term because of his violence towards his wife and the poor woman could stand no more. His mother coped as well as she could. She was in the habit of taking him to a neighbour, a Mrs Goddard, who seemed to be able to calm him down when he grew too violent. But on Saturday night even Mrs Goddard had difficulty coping with him and she went back with them to Mrs Drant's cottage. Drant seemed very depressed and kept saying that he was dying.

'You must pray to the lord for help, William,' said Mrs Goddard.

'I have been praying,' he snapped back. Then he subsided into a chair. But he wasn't still for long. He jumped up and raised his hand to strike Mrs Goddard.

She raised her hand to ward off the blow. 'Don't William! We have been friends for so long.'

Drant lowered his arm, then shouted, 'All this week you've been trying to poison me!'

Mrs Drant, who could see that her son was turning violent, took the opportunity to rush out of the cottage door into the street outside. But Drant, seeing his mother go, turned his attentions to her and ran out after her. Mrs Goddard could hear the sounds of shouting outside and the screams of Mrs Drant, and a moment later Drant came back in, dragging his mother by the scruff of her neck, and threw her down on the floor. All the commotion had raised the neighbours, even though it was eleven o'clock at night and most of them had been in bed. A couple of women, Mrs Burgess and Mrs Fell, poked their heads in the cottage door and then rushed away to obtain help, in fear that Drant would murder his mother.

They first called on the parish constable, Thomas Gell, since he lived nearest, and he got out of bed, asking his wife to wake up their son, William, as they would both go to Drant's cottage. Then the two women went on to a farm where William Marshall lived with his mother. He also hurriedly dressed and came to the Drant cottage, meeting the Gells as he arrived at the door. At the cottage they were met by a staggering sight. William Drant had his mother spread-eagled on the floor and was kneeling on her chest, a knife in his hand, and shouting that he was going to kill her.

Marshall approached him and said in a conciliatory voice, 'Now, Billy, what are you up to? Let your mother get up.'

'Stand back!' shouted the crazed blacksmith. 'If you come any gainer I'll stab you.'

Several people tried to reason with Drant, but Marshall thought it best if he went to fetch reinforcements so that they might overcome the raging man. He therefore quickly left and went to a neighbouring farm owned by a John Graves and asked him to come and help; they were joined by Reuben Leggett, another blacksmith in the village. They all crowded into the small cottage room where Drant was still shouting and waving his knife about: 'If you come any nearer,' he warned them, 'I'll rip your guts out!'

When Marshall came too near, Drant slashed at his leg with the knife. Luckily Marshall was wearing gaiters: the knife cut through the leather and his trousers underneath, but did not succeed in touching the skin. At this Thomas Gell shouted, 'On to him lads!' And they all closed in. Graves had brought a length of timber with him, part of a fence post, and he hit Drant over the head with it, while the others threw themselves on top of the man on the floor.

He was still fighting like a mad man, but they managed to roll him off his mother so that the hysterical woman was able to scramble to her feet and rush out of the cottage door to seek shelter with a neighbour. Thomas Gell had by this time managed to disarm Drant and secure the clasp knife himself, and he ordered the rest of the men to leave the cottage. They all knew that these episodes of Drant's violence did not usually last long, and they assumed that the fit would soon abate in this case.

But Drant was not done yet. When they released him and turned to leave he got to his feet, picked up the fencepost that Graves had dropped and swung it at Reuben Leggett, who was nearest him. He missed but such was force of his swing that he overbalanced and went down on his knees on the floor. The others took the opportunity to run out of the cottage into the darkness. William Gell then realised that his father was not with them and turned back to see him come out of the cottage door and into the night. The enraged Drant came after them and in the confusion and the darkness none of them really saw what happened next: William Gell said later that he saw someone fall, but he could not tell who it was. It seems likely however that it was Thomas Gell who, with only one eye, could probably not see properly and tripped over something in the dark. As he lay on the ground, Drant came up behind him and belaboured him with his balk of wood. Leggett said afterwards that he saw Drant standing over the stricken man and several others said that they heard blows being struck. And Mrs Burgess heard Drant say, 'You b——, I'll give it to you!' She hurried round to the house of the parish constable to tell Mrs Gell that she thought her husband might be hurt, and Mrs Gell ran out to where a crowd had gathered around the man on the ground. She was in tears when she came back, and said to Mrs Burgess: 'Come and help me. My master is dying.'

By this time police constable John Lawson, who was a regular policeman in the Lincolnshire Force stationed at the nearby village of Baumber, had been summoned. He found the injured man not far from Drant's cottage and took a light from William Gell to examine the victim. He discovered that Thomas Gell had a huge wound at the back of his

Coach and Horses in 1950s. (Courtesy K. Stride)

St Margaret's church.
(Hemingby Pictures,
L10 10 398)

head, but was not dead, although he couldn't speak when Lawson asked who had hit him. The policeman supervised the transporting of Thomas Gell back to his own home. Mrs Gell and Mrs Burgess had found a board and placed it on a two-wheeled trolley and the injured man was lifted on to it and wheeled back to his own cottage. Then Lawson went to Drant's cottage.

The man was standing in the doorway of his cottage brandishing the 4ft balk of timber. 'Keep off! I'll kill the first b—— that comes near me!'

'Now then Drant. What have you been up to?'

'Keep off. I don't want to hurt you, but if you come here I'll kill you!'

But PC Lawson was a brave man. He took out his truncheon and prepared to rush the burly blacksmith, who was waving his large piece of wood. But as he did so, Drant slipped inside his cottage and tried to close the door behind him. The policeman, however, was quicker and shoved his truncheon into the gap left between the door and the jamb. Then, helped by other villagers, he was able to force open the cottage door. He closed with Drant and wrestled him to the floor, where he put handcuffs on him. Then he picked up the piece of wood Drant had been waving and saw that there was blood and grey hair on it. By this time William Gell had gone to Horncastle to get hold of a doctor (or surgeon, as they were called in those days). He came back with Mr Arthur Boulton, who went immediately to Thomas Gell's cottage, but it was only to pronounce the man dead.

William Drant was taken to the lock-up in Horncastle and eventually charged with murder at the police station. He is reported to have said, 'Oh dear. I did not think that I had killed him.' And he then burst into tears. When asked why he had done it he replied, 'the men were hounding me while I did not know what I was doing and I had to get rid of them.'

The inquest was held at the Coach and Horses public house in the village and as was usual the jury, after being sworn-in, were taken to view the body and the place where the assault took place. John Graves, William Marshall, Reuben Leggett, William Gell and Mrs Burgess all gave their versions of what had happened that night. Mr Arthur Boulton, the surgeon, reported that on a post-mortem examination he found that Gell's skull had

Thomas Bett Gell's grave in St Margaret's churchyard. (Hemingby Pictures RFD 8210)

been broken into seven pieces. The injuries sustained could have been the result of several blows but he was of the opinion that his skull had been fractured by the first blow, which would have been enough to have killed him eventually. The coroner summed up, and the jury, without retiring to consider, brought in a verdict of wilful murder.

Drant went before the magistrates in Horncastle, in the police station instead of the police court, on the following Wednesday. He was duly committed for trial at the next assizes in Lincoln. Meanwhile, the funeral of Thomas Gell had taken place the preceding day at St Margaret's church. Practically the whole village turned out, as Gell had been a popular man; the service was conducted by the previous vicar, who had now retired. He was George Thackeray, cousin to the famous author William Makepeace Thackeray, author of *Vanity Fair*. He had been in the living since 1840.

William Drant went to trial at Lincoln on Monday, 27 December 1876, before Mr Baron Huddleston. The prosecution was led by Mr Buzzard and Mr Lumley and the defence was in the hands of Mr Horace Smith. He pleaded insanity for the prisoner, but he was bound at the time by the McNaghten Rules: they said that a verdict of 'not guilty through insanity' could only be reached if a defendant did not know the nature and quality of his act; or if he did know this he didn't know that it was wrong. This was an extremely difficult thing to prove, and many people went to the gallows then who today we would undoubtedly say were insane. The only way a defendant could avoid hanging was if the jury brought in a verdict of manslaughter in which the intention to kill was absent.

The judge summed up largely against Drant saying that the law presumed all killing to be murder and it was up to the accused to show that the offence was manslaughter only. He obviously swayed the jury, who brought in a verdict after only half an hour's deliberation of guilty of murder. The judge put on the black cap and sentenced the prisoner to death.

But the case had attracted national publicity and was reported in *The Times*. Henry Maudsley, a leading psychiatrist, wrote to the newspapers about the neglected aspects of epilepsy and pointed out that Drant's mother was one of the best people to give evidence of his condition, and she had said, 'he usually went violent after these fits. During the time he was in the house on that fateful night he was talking to himself. I washed him about seven o'clock when he was trembling violently and seemed to know nothing.' And Maudsley wrote that William Drant's case was a classic example of the ravages of the disease.

Horncastle Market Square.

Maudsley's writings seemed to have either stirred up similar feelings in the village or mirrored opinions which were already there, since William Drant had been born and brought up in the village and must have been known to a large number of people there. After the trial, a petition was raised in the village and the surrounding area calling for a reprieve for the prisoner. This was eventually granted and Drant was detained 'during Her Majesty's pleasure'.

Henry Maudsley went on to found a research centre into mental illness. And at the London hospital which bears his name, some research was done which showed that of a large number of people convicted of murder, a high proportion of them suffered from epilepsy; far more than in the general population.

Six

A DROWNING IN THE FOSSDYKE

Hannah Wright, 1895

Early in the morning of Tuesday, 27 August 1895 a labourer named Frederick Brown was walking to work along the bank of the Fossdyke Canal near the Brayford Pool in Lincoln. He worked on the new railway line being constructed near Pye Wipe. As he walked he glanced at the water and saw what looked like a child's shirt floating on the surface. The place was just opposite the rear of the grandstand of the racecourse. He went to a nearby hedge to cut a stick, reasoning that the shirt cleaned up might do for one of his own children. He bent over the bank and used the stick to reach the shirt. But he found it hard to move. And the stick broke. Then suddenly a dark shape surfaced and he found himself looking at the back of a child's head. The shirt contained the body of a child.

He jerked upright in horror and looked about him. He wasn't far from the nearest signal box on a regular line nearby, and he raced along to it and breathlessly burst out his story to the signalman. The signalman told him to run to the nearest police station, and in the meantime he told a porter who worked at the Pye Wipe Junction on the Great Northern Railway to go to the place where Brown had seen the body. The porter, whose name was Ernest Rippon, duly found the place and, using a larger stick this time, managed to pull the body to the bank. He carefully lifted it out of the water and laid it on the grass. It was a young child and clearly dead, because the body was cold. The body was of a male child; it was wearing only a calico night shirt which had been crocheted at the edges. He looked to be between three and four years old.

Eventually two policemen turned up, constables Milner and Cooke, and they carried the body to the police station. Later that day Ernest Rippon found some child's boots and socks in the hedge bottom near where the body had been discovered. Dr McFarland was called to the police station and he examined the body. He reported that the child was 33ins in length and weighed 25lbs. He had dark brown hair and blue eyes and his arms and face were sunburnt. The doctor performed a post-mortem examination on the body and said that there were no external signs of violence, except for an injury on the left shin which might, he thought, have been caused during play. The body was that of a well-nourished child who had no disease and the cause of death was drowning. These findings were confirmed by a Dr Peacock who said that he had never seen a more perfectly developed child. He thought the boy was three years old.

The Chief Constable of the Lincoln Constabulary, Mr Mansell, suggested that the body should be photographed to help with identification and this was done. The police also thought that it was not impossible that the mother might also have drowned in the canal, and it was dragged for several hours on Tuesday afternoon; no body was found. But late on the Tuesday afternoon a young man appeared at the police station in Lincoln, and he had a curious story to tell.

He was James Fenton and he lived in Danesgate. He said that he had been on the Foss bank at about 9.30 p.m. on the previous evening with his girlfriend. A young woman passed them carrying a bundle in her arms. She was a pretty woman, and as far they could tell looked to be in her early twenties. As she passed they both heard a whimpering coming from the bundle, and Fenton said to his girlfriend, 'That sounds like a child.' But the woman hurried past and they heard nothing further from the bundle. They carried on walking and sometime later, when they were saying goodnight, the woman passed them again, but walking in the opposite direction. And this time she did not have a bundle in her arms.

'That's very strange,' said Fenton to his companion. 'I'm sure the woman had a parcel in her arms when she passed us the first time and it sounded like a child in it. But now she hasn't got the parcel.'

'Whatever do you think she's done with it?'

Fossdyke Canal in Lincoln.

Fenton shook his head. 'I don't know. She might have given the child to someone else who we didn't see.'

'Or she might have left the child somewhere. Or,' and her face turned grave, 'she might have thrown it into the water!'

'Do you really think so?'

'Well, what other explanation is there? We haven't seen anyone else around, have we?' She looked after the retreating figure of the woman. 'Don't you think you ought to go and ask her what she's done with the baby?'

Fenton looked extremely uncomfortable. With all the Englishman's natural aversion to making a scene, he didn't want to go and tackle the woman. But on the other hand he felt that he ought to do something. 'I'll follow her,' he compromised.

His companion looked at him in disgust. 'Well, if you're not going to go and speak to her, I'm going home. I'm not trailing about at this time of night. My parents will be wondering where I am.' She waited a moment to see if he would offer to see her home, but he didn't; he kept looking after the woman. She shrugged her shoulders and left. Fenton stood for a moment undecided, but then, as if dragged along by some invisible string binding him to the woman, he followed her. They went through various streets and up the very steep hill, Fenton keeping a fair distance behind her so that should she turn he would be able to dive into a doorway. But she seemed preoccupied and did not look round. It turned out that he was really too far behind, because when he saw her turn into a street and he reached the end of it himself she had disappeared. He reasoned, however, that she must have gone into one of the houses in the street and he looked for the street name. It was Alexandra Terrace.

The police also received some more information about the mysterious woman. John Hobbins, a butcher who lived in Carr Street, near the Fossdyke, also saw her on Monday night. He had a field with some cattle in it, nearby, and he was going to check on them when he saw the young woman by the Foss bank. She was walking up and down with the child in her arms. The child appeared to be crying and she was trying to comfort it. He went on to his field and when he returned a short time later he saw the woman again. This time she was sitting down on the footpath by the canal, near to Carr Street. She still had the child in her arms, but when she saw him she got up and walked away towards Lincoln.

The police made house to house enquiries in Alexandra Terrace. In those days it was only a short street with few houses in it and as with many small street communities everybody knew everyone else's business. It wasn't long before they heard of a young woman lodging at 23 Alexandra Terrace with her brother and his wife and three children. The young woman herself was reputed to have a child of her own, but she kept it with a baby minder in the village of Weston in Nottinghamshire, some twelve miles to the west of Lincoln. The police duly sent off a photograph of the child taken from the Fossdyke to Weston and by the next day, Wednesday, they had confirmation that it was the same child.

The young woman was in fact Hannah Elizabeth Wright, and she had only recently begun lodging at 23 Alexandra Terrace with her brother William and her sister-in-law Jane. Hannah was twenty-three years of age. She had been in domestic service in Weston and about three years ago there she had an illegitimate child, a boy called Albert Edward Wright. On Sunday, 25 August 1895, Hannah arrived at her brother's house to take afternoon tea. She told her sister-in-law that she had been staying with some friends in either Duke Street or Canon Street. Jane could not afterwards remember exactly which. Hannah had with her a young man called Spurr from Branston, a village just outside Lincoln. They remained until about six o'clock and then left. Hannah returned the next day, Monday, alone at about noon. She stayed for only about half an hour and then said she was going to Branston. She said that she had been in service there with a Mr Marshall until the week before. But now she was hoping to go into service in Hykeham.

But in reality, Hannah went to Weston that afternoon and, according to Miss Jane Flear, who had been looking after young Albert Wright, she took the child away with her, saying that she had a new situation to go to and would have the child with her. To the surprise of Miss Flear, however, she did not take the child's clothes, saying that she was going to buy him some new things.

Hannah returned to her brother's home after ten o'clock on Monday night. Again she was alone. 'You're a bit late aren't you?' asked William.

'Yes, I've been for a long walk.'

Jane Wright thought she seemed a little tense. 'Will you have some supper, Hannah?'

'No thank you. But I'll have a glass of beer, if I may.'

Jane brought her the beer and Hannah drank it greedily. 'Is that your young man?' asked Jane, referring to the young man who had been with her the day before.

'Yes. We are going to get married when he can find a house for us in Branston.'

'Where's young Albert? Have you left him with Miss Flear in Weston?'

Hannah nodded and went on drinking her beer.

'What about young Spurr. Does he know about Albert?' asked Jane.

Hannah shook her head. 'No, he doesn't and I'm not going to tell him either.'

Alexandra Terrace in Lincoln.

Carr Street, Lincoln.

Jane was surprised. 'Well, I think that is very wrong, Hannah. You can't marry the man and not tell him about your son. He'll be bound to find out sooner or later and it will only be stirring up trouble for yourself.'

'I'm not going to tell him and that's the end of it. Some people in Nottingham are going to adopt him and he will never know anything about him.'

This of course was a considerable dilemma for Hannah. At the time there were few men who would consider marrying a woman who had a child. For many men the ideal was to marry a virgin and the idea that she had already been with a man would be repugnant. In those days the prevalent attitude to men was quite different. A man would be forgiven – probably even it would be expected – if he had sexual relations with a woman before he was married. But women were not allowed such latitude. It would be even worse to learn that the woman had a child out of wedlock. She would then be regarded as little more than a common prostitute.

Hannah and Jane agreed not to argue further about it and the family went to bed. Hannah left the next morning, saying she was going to see some friends. But she didn't return that night. The next day, Wednesday, a police detective called at 23 Alexandra Terrace. He asked to see Hannah. Jane said that she did not know where she was and asked what it was all about. The detective was not very forthcoming, but he did explain that the body of a young child had been found in the Fossdyke Canal and they were questioning young women who were known to have young children. Jane was shocked to hear the news and a horrible suspicion began to take hold of her mind.

When Hannah finally came back that Wednesday, Jane was clearly distraught. 'Hannah, there's been a policeman here to see you. Apparently a young child has been found drowned in the Fossdyke and they're asking all young women who have children. Tell me quickly it's not you. I've been in a terrible state ever since he came.'

'It's not me, Jane.'

'Oh, what a relief! I've been like a cat on hot bricks all day. That's all right then, because he's coming back to see you and you will be able to put him straight.' But when she looked at Hannah she could see the tears running down the young woman's face.

'I can't, Jane. It's me.'

'Oh my God! The Lord preserve us!' Jane sat down in a chair and put her head in her hands. When she raised her face to look again at Hannah she saw that the young woman had wiped her face and the tears appeared to have gone. Jane gulped. 'Hannah, what... what did you do it for?'

Hannah drew out a chair and sat opposite Jane. Now she seemed quite composed. She shrugged her shoulders. 'I just couldn't manage anymore on my own. The people at Weston keep complaining that it is a great deal of trouble to them to keep little Albert. And they want three shillings and sixpence a week now and I simply can't afford it.'

'But why didn't you come to us, Hannah? Tell your brother about it. We would have managed somehow.'

Hannah shrugged her shoulders again. 'I don't know. Didn't want to bother William I suppose. But it's over and done with now. I suppose I'd better go to the police and tell them about it, so they know. Then I can get on with my life.'

'But Hannah, it's a very serious business. You've killed a child.'

'Yes I know. But it had to be done. I couldn't look after it any longer.' She got to her feet. 'I'll just pop down to the police station, tell them about it.' She looked up. 'I wonder what the time is? I've got to be at my new situation tonight.'

High Street, Branston village.

Jane was appalled that Hannah seemed to be taking it all so calmly and didn't realise the seriousness of her situation. 'I'm sorry, Hannah. I can't come with you as I've got to collect the children from school. But I'll go next door and see if Mrs Close will go with you to the police station.'

'All right. But don't tell everyone in the street. I don't want it talked about.'

Mrs Sarah Close agreed to go with Hannah to the police station and on the way Hannah told Mrs Close what had happened. 'I wonder what will happen to me,' mused Hannah. 'Do you think I might have to pay something?'

'I don't know,' replied an astonished Mrs Close.

When they reached the police station they were taken to see Inspector Basham. In the presence of the Inspector and Mrs Close Hannah said, 'I've come to give myself up for killing my child.' She was cautioned and she then made the following statement:

I am a domestic servant and have been living at Mr Marshall's in Branston, but have been staying with my brother at 23 Alexandra Terrace since Friday last. On Monday night a little after nine o'clock I went down by Brayford and threw it into the water and went back to my brother's directly.

This confession was used at Hannah's trial. The defence put forward the contention that Hannah was suffering from temporary insanity. Mrs Jane Wright said that she thought her sister-in-law was a bit simple in some things and had not the thoughtfulness one would expect to find in one her age. 'No woman in her right mind,' protested the defence counsel 'could believe that she could make such a confession and then be allowed to go home.' But the judge, Mr Justice Day, rejected the plea of insanity. 'It might be true,' he said, 'that the woman is simple-minded. But simple-mindedness is not insanity. A more premeditated murder of a child has never been my duty to try.'

The jury took the hint and brought in a verdict of guilty of murder, but they also gave a strong recommendation to mercy. The judge said he would pass on the recommendation, but he had no alternative but to sentence her to death. But there was a strong feeling in Lincoln that she should not hang and a petition was raised, which was signed by the bishop of Lincoln, the mayor and deputy mayor and many industrialists in the town. Five days after the trial she was reprieved, and sentenced to life imprisonment.

Seven

'I NEVER THOUGHT IT WOULD COME TO THIS'

Joseph Bowser, 1897

Donington is a small town in the fens lying west of Boston and some eighteen miles south east of Lincoln. It was listed in the Domesday Book of 1087 as 'Donnictune' and had extensive salt works since in winter much of the land around was inundated by the sea and the area was known as the wet or salt fen. It was once important for flax and hemp production, but is now better known as one of the centres of the tulip industry. Its importance as a market town in medieval times is shown by its imposing church, St Mary and the Holy Rood. But its main claim to fame must be as the birth place of Matthew Flinders.

Captain Matthew Flinders RN was born in the town on 16 March 1774 and educated at the Cowley School in the town and at the grammar school in Horbling (about halfway between Donington and Grantham). His family were local doctors and it was expected that he would go into the medical profession, but after reading *Robinson Crusoe* he is said to have been fired to go exploring. He joined the navy in 1789 and in 1791 sailed under Captain Bligh to transport breadfruit trees from Tahiti to the West Indies; in 1795 he sailed to Port Jackson, the natural harbour of Sydney, Australia. After carrying out several expeditions to explore the coast around Port Jackson, he returned to England and proposed a circumnavigation of Australia to survey the complete coast.

This was enthusiastically supported by Sir Joseph Banks, whose home was at Revesby Abbey near Horncastle, and who had accompanied Captain Cook on one of his expeditions to the South Seas. Sir Joseph Banks was President of the Royal Society and he helped raise money for the project. Flinders set off in 1801. By 1802 he had surveyed the southern and eastern coast of the continent and passed through the Torres Strait to the north into the Gulf of Carpentaria. But the vessel began to leak and Flinders decided to abandon the surveying, but to return to Sydney by the western coast, thus circumnavigating the continent, the first time this had been done. The vessel could not be repaired and Flinders had to return to England by another vessel. War between England and France had broken

Northorpe village.

out again and when he reached Mauritius, under French control, he was imprisoned there. He spent six years in captivity, but spent his time writing his major work *A Voyage to Terra Australis*. He was released in 1810 and completed his book, which was published in April 1814, just a few days before his early death at just forty. His memorial is in the church at Donington and in commemoration of his work the Australian Government sends representatives to make an annual pilgrimage to Lincolnshire in early March.

But Donington has another place in history, though this time not such a celebrated one. To the north of the town lies the small hamlet of Northorpe; today it almost joins the town. On the morning of Tuesday, 25 March 1897 a servant girl at one of the farmhouses there got up early. She was sixteen-year-old Elizabeth Berridge and she had only worked at the farmhouse since the previous Friday, but already she was beginning to understand why her master and mistress had difficulty keeping servants.

Her master, Joseph Bowser, was a big beefy man of forty-three who weighed in the region of fifteen stones and had a black bushy beard and moustache. His face was red, and he had a bulbous nose which was already showing the signs of being a heavy drinker. But he was a well-known and successful farmer in the district. He rented the farm he lived on from a Captain Gleed, but he also rented two other farms in the neighbourhood of Bridge End, Donington, and a further one at Wyberton, near Boston. He had been for a number of years one of the three representatives from Donington of the Spalding Board of Guardians (the governors of the local workhouse) and had also been active in the administration of the Poor Law in Donington.

He had married Susan Harrison eleven years before and they had no children. Susan was a widow when she married Joseph; she came originally from New Bolingbroke, and her maiden name was Brummitt. She had married her first husband, Harrison, and had a son by him. At the time of the tragedy, her son lived in Lincoln. Harrison subsequently died, and Susan went to work as a housekeeper for Joseph. Then, after about a year, they married.

Donnington sign.

But the marriage, latterly, had not been a happy one. Both of them were strong willed, and there were frequent rows. Joseph's behaviour had also changed considerably after he had been thrown out of a gig on to his head. Both Susan and Joseph were very heavy drinkers. Young Elizabeth Drury was Joseph Bowser's niece. She lived at Wyberton, and she said that she didn't like visiting her uncle's house because of his drinking and his fearful temper. In fact, she was actually afraid of him. She also said she had seen Susan Bowser drunk as well. About a year before, Susan had left Joseph because of his drinking and his violence. But he prevailed upon her to come back, and they were apparently reconciled.

On that fateful Tuesday in March, Elizabeth Berridge was the only servant in the farmhouse. She was up before daylight to light the fires and make the breakfast for her master, who rose at six o'clock. Her mistress got up soon afterwards, but relations between her and Joseph were not cordial over breakfast. Joseph went out after breakfast to see to his stock and to give his only farm worker, James Collishaw, his orders for the day. James too had only started to work at the farm that day. Bowser returned to the farmhouse at about ten o'clock and went up to his room, and Elizabeth saw no more of him until about three o'clock in the afternoon. He had apparently spent the time drinking, since the servant saw his wife take some whisky up to him.

At about twelve o'clock Elizabeth made a meal for Susan and the farm-hand, and for Eliza Drury, making one of her rare visits to the farmhouse. Eliza was accompanied by her cousin Fred Lister, who was Joseph's nephew. Fred was leaving for Cape Town in a few days, having obtained a job in South Africa, and they both went up to see Bowser so that Fred could say goodbye to his uncle. Then the two young people went for a walk. About 4.30 p.m. Bowser came downstairs. He was visibly but not staggeringly drunk. He asked Elizabeth where his wife was and she told him that she was outside feeding the chickens. He went outside. Susan was mixing the feed and he asked her what she was doing. She apparently told him; in response he kicked her in the back, and she fell to the ground.

This may sound like an unprovoked attack, and it may well have been. However, on the other hand it is quite possible that, when her husband asked what she was doing, she might easily have said something like, 'What does it look like?'

However it started, this seemed to be the culmination of a long-held resentment and resulted in a fury which would know no bounds. Susan got up, and Joseph attacked her again, following her as she tried to get away into a nearby field. She tried to hide behind a tumbrel (a farm cart made famous by being used to transport prisoners to the guillotine in the French Revolution) in the middle of the field, but he pursued her, kicking her repeatedly, until she collapsed, unable to move.

All this had been seen by a farm worker in a nearby field, and also by Eliza Drury and Fred Lister, who were coming back from their walk. When they got back to the farmhouse, Joseph was sitting in the kitchen by the fire. Neither of them seems to have said anything to him. Elizabeth Berridge came into the kitchen and began to lay the table for tea. As the two young people sat down at the table she asked Bowser if he wanted any food. He shook his head. Then he got up and left the room, but before he left he said to Lister: 'Never be married.' The two carried on with their meal. Bowser returned after a few minutes and took down his double-barrelled shotgun from the wall above the fireplace. He said to Lister: 'Have you got any cartridges?' The young man said he had not. Bowser went to the kitchen window and took down a cartridge that was lying on the sill. As he put it in his gun he muttered: 'I'll shoot her. She'll not aggravate me anymore!' Then he left to go into an inner room to get another cartridge.

The two young people sat as if transfixed, saying nothing but looking at each other in horror. But Elizabeth Berridge was made of sterner stuff. Showing remarkable courage, she rushed out of the house to tell her mistress of the danger and to entreat her come into the house. Susan Bowser had by this time staggered as far as the calf shed. 'Come in mistress! Come in! Master's got his gun!' But she was too late, for Joseph had come up behind her.

He pointed the gun at his wife. 'Now you may look out for it!'

Donnington Market Square.

Donnington.

But his hand was unsteady as he pointed the gun. Elizabeth had taken hold of her mistress's hand and Susan hauled herself upright, leaning against the door of the calf shed. She lifted her head, 'You can do it!' she croaked.

Joseph pulled the trigger. There was a loud report and the wood in the door above Susan's head shattered. But she was unharmed. He pulled the next trigger – but this time the shot hit home. It caught Susan in the side of the head and she went down by the side of the door without a sound. Elizabeth screamed, but Joseph took no notice and went back towards the house. Elizabeth looked down at her mistress and realised that she was dead; she followed Joseph into the house.

Joseph came into the kitchen and said to the two young people still sitting immobile at the kitchen table, 'I've just shot her.'

Eliza Drury turned to Elizabeth. 'Is that true?'

Elizabeth said that it was, and the two young people hurried out to see for themselves. When Eliza saw that Susan was indeed dead, she went immediately for a neighbour, a Joe Gunson, who was also her uncle. They returned and found Bowser in the farmyard in an excitable state.

'What's happed to your wife?' asked Joe Gunson.

'She's against the calf house door. Go and look.'

Gunson did so and was followed by Bowser. 'Oh, Joseph!' cried Gunson, 'I never thought it would come to this.'

'She tantalised me and aggravated me. And she dared me to do it!'

Then Bowser went to the granary and shouted up the granary ladder to Collishaw, who was in the loft. 'Jim, come here. Harness the horse and go and fetch the police inspector and the doctor.' He went back into the kitchen followed by Collishaw. Bowser saw

St Mary's church, Donnington.

Fred Lister and Eliza Drury there. He turned to Collishaw. 'Don't bother harnessing the horse.' Then he turned to Lister. 'Would you telegraph for the inspector and the doctor and my two brothers?' Then he sat down heavily by the fire. 'I wish I could shoot myself, but I can't.'

When Inspector Davey and Dr Jellye from Donington arrived and the doctor had examined Susan, Bowser said to him. 'Oh Doctor. I've done it this time. Your medicine is no use now.' The inspector cautioned Bowser and said that he was arresting him on suspicion of him having murdered his wife. 'That's right,' said Bowser, 'and there's the gun I did it with.' He pointed to a gun on the kitchen sofa.

The inspector examined the gun. He could tell that both barrels had been fired, but there was still an undischarged cartridge in one of them. This pointed to the fact that Bowser might well have thought about killing himself, but hadn't the nerve to do it.

Bowser was tried at Lincoln Assizes on 7 July, 1897 before Mr Justice Pollock. Mr Appleton led the prosecution and Bowser was defended by Mr Stanger. The defence tried to suggest that Susan had contributed to her demise by her own drunken behaviour, but the judge said that this could not justify murder. Medical experts rejected the defence assertion that Bowser's actions were occasioned by insanity or epilepsy and put his wild behaviour down to drink. The jury took only half an hour to bring in a verdict of guilty of murder and Joseph Bowser was condemned to death. During his stay in Lincoln Prison he had a relatively comfortable cell, having one of the association cells rather than the usual condemned cell. He was also allowed plenty of food and put on 20lbs in weight. He thus required only a short drop when he was executed by James Billington on 27 July in the Greetwell Road Prison.

Eight

A FATAL AFFRAY

Joseph Bones, 1866

When the Lincolnshire fens were drained in the late eighteenth century, many new waterways were made and some old streams canalised. One of these was the Billinghay Skirt which ran from the Sleaford canal north to join up with the River Witham. Today the A153 from Louth to Sleaford largely follows the waterway, beyond Tattershall Bridge (which crosses the Witham), and the village of Billinghay clusters around the waterway and a minor road which leads off the A153. It is mentioned in the Domesday Book, and would have been in olden times a settlement on a gravel mound surrounded by marshland, usually flooded in winter. With the draining of the fens much high-quality farmland was produced, and in the 1860s Billinghay was a substantial village with well over 2,000 inhabitants and nearly 500 dwellings. There were two pubs, the Cross Keys and the Golden Cross, and a substantial parish church. This was dedicated to St Michael and All Angels and dated from the thirteenth century. The church has a slender spire linked to the old tower by flying buttresses and can be seen from miles away in the flat country which surrounds it. Since it was an agricultural village, Billinghay had many trades associated with farming, and not the least of these would have been the blacksmiths needed for the making and

Billinghay Skirt.

repair of agricultural implements, the shoeing of horses and the upkeep of farm carts and wagons.

There were three blacksmiths in the village, and one was called Joseph Benton. He had a forge on the main street of the village and employed several men in his establishment. On Thursday morning, 16 August 1866, he had two men working: Eyre Petchell and Thomas Farnsworth. At about twelve o'clock that morning another man came into the shop. He was forty-four-year-old Joseph Bones. Bones had a reputation in the village as a violent and unpredictable man. By many accounts he was also extraordinarily ugly, with facial features which were irregular – to say the least. This may have contributed to his abrasiveness, but as we shall see there may have been an underlying cause of his violence. He was obviously in a bad mood, as he began abusing the staff (though what he actually said is not recorded). He might have had an underlying grievance against the blacksmith or members of his team; or he might have been spoiling for a fight, for a reason best known to him; he may have wanted to stir up animosity. Whatever the reason was, Joseph Benton became fed up with it and told Bones to leave. Most blacksmiths were big, heavily built men: Benton probably was too, which accounts for the fact that Bones did not decide to take him on. With a muttered curse he turned away, but as he was leaving surreptitiously picked up a piece of wood. As he walked by Thomas Farnsworth, a younger and much slimmer man, he swung the club at him.

But Farnsworth had been watching Bones out of the corner of his eye and as the older man swung the wood at his head he dodged out of the way. This caused Bones to swing off balance as the blow sailed harmlessly over Farnsworth's head. It also gave the younger man the opportunity to jump on Bones' back and force him to the floor. He grabbed the man's arm as he did so, and twisted it up behind Bones' back. Bones began yelling for help, shouting that he was being attacked and killed. But the rest of the men in the blacksmith's shop ignored his cries. Farnsworth then forced the older man to his feet and marched him out of the door and into the street, where he released him with a shove. Bones went staggering across the road before he regained his balance. Then he turned. But he could see young Farnsworth standing in the doorway opposite, arms akimbo, waiting for him to come back and receive further treatment. He decided to break off the engagement and with a few more curses he went into another blacksmith's shop, which was just opposite Joseph Benton's.

It seems likely that he tried the same thing in the other blacksmith's shop, since it wasn't long before he came out of there. But this time he began his attack on Joseph Benton's shop by calling for Farnsworth to come out and face him 'like a man' – and throwing stones at him when he appeared. In those days the roads were little more than dirt tracks, beaten down by the pressure of many feet, the hooves of horses and the wheels of carts, and there would have been plenty of stones lying around. This may seem like childish behaviour for a forty-four-year-old man, but it does show something of his state of mind. Too afraid to take on the young man physically, but still furious at being humiliated by him, the only approach he could think of was to pursue the attack from a distance.

But again, he had reckoned without the young man's retaliation. Farnsworth rushed out of the blacksmith's shop, crossed the road and grappled with Bones before the older man could pick up another stone. Bones was no match for the stronger and younger man

St Michael and All Angels' church, Billinghay.

and he found himself thrown to the ground again, with Farnsworth on top of him. Bones began yelling and calling for help, shouting that the younger man would surely kill him. This, of course, attracted a crowd of onlookers, and some young men raced up shouting for Farnsworth to leave the older man alone. What then might have developed into a free-for-all, with a great number of men becoming involved, was fortunately scotched by another man coming out of Benton's shop.

Eyre Petchell was carrying a large baulk of timber in his hand. 'Clear off,' he shouted to the crowd of young men, 'it's no business of yours!'

They looked at him and at the piece of wood he was swinging at his side and decided that perhaps they wouldn't join in. They slunk off.

'Let him get up, Thomas,' said Petchell, 'if he puts down the stone he has in his hand.'

'Ya!' shouted Bones at Petchell, 'You can't do anything without having that wood in your hand.' But at the same time he dropped the stone.

Petchell put down the baulk of wood and Farnsworth got up from the ground, allowing Bones to get up also. Both Petchell and Farnsworth then thought that that would be the end of the matter, and they turned to go back to the blacksmith's shop. They did not see Bones put his hand in his pocket and bring it out with a folding pocket knife. It had two blades and he flicked out the larger blade. 'Come on, then,' he shouted, 'see how brave you are now!' And he began waving the knife about in sweeping gestures. At this, the crowd that had collected to watch retreated to a safe distance. Farnsworth and Petchell, realising that they could not cope with a knife-wielding man like Bones, raced away too.

Next door to the blacksmith's shop was the house of Mr Short. His door was open as he had heard the racket outside and had come out to see what the matter was. He was standing by his door and he beckoned the two to come into his house. Farnsworth was in the lead and he rushed into Mrs Short's house and, forgetting that Petchell was following, shut the door behind him. Petchell thus had to go round the back of the house to hide.

Bones did not follow them. He merely stood in the road shouting for them to come out and face him. As far as he was concerned, he had won the battle. His enemies had fled before him and he was going to make the most of it. Petchell could hear him shouting

Billinghay.

from behind Mr Short's house and he waited a while, but eventually could stand it no longer: something would have to be done to end this situation. However, he was afraid to just slink away and hope that Bones would eventually get tired of shouting in the street and go home. There were plenty of villagers standing around whom he knew, and he didn't want to appear cowardly in their eyes.

'All right,' he shouted. 'I'm coming out! I'm not afraid of you, Bones!' And he came round the side of the house and walked out into the street and up to the shouting man. Most onlookers didn't see the knife, but only Bones' arm as he quickly stepped forward and slashed upwards with the blade. Petchell reeled back and cried: 'He's done me!' Bones shouted in triumph: 'That'll cool you, you b——!' Petchell lurched back, and the watchers could now see that the front of his smock (most labourers in those days wore a long smock) was covered in blood. He staggered away and, helped by several other men, tottered into Mr Short's house.

Bones still stood in the middle of the road waving his bloodstained knife about. He seemed proud and pleased at what he had done. 'I sharpened this,' he said to the crowd, indicating the knife, 'only this morning. And it's done a great job.' A man named Palmer tried to approach, but Bones waved the knife in his face. 'Come any nearer and you'll get the same!' But then he seemed to tire of his success and he calmly folded up the knife and put it in his pocket. This was the moment the crowd had been waiting for, and several men closed in and grabbed him. He began struggling but they held him tightly. Clarke Enderby, who had been one of the bystanders, put his hand in Bones' pocket and retrieved the knife, which he subsequently handed over to the parish constable.

Joseph Benton, who had followed the stricken Eyre Petchell into Mr Short's house, now saw that his employee had a huge wound in his abdomen and his intestines were hanging out. He quickly went for medical assistance. Ebenezer Thompson, who was the local doctor, came quickly and bound up the wound. When he was asked what the situation looked like, he shook his head: 'His bowels are cut through. He won't recover.' And he didn't. Eyre Petchell died the next morning.

Golden Cross, Billinghay, with the bridge over the Skirt and the church in the background.

Meanwhile, William Knowles the parish constable had found Bones at home and arrested him. When he was apprehended Bones said, 'I know I have done it and I will do the same to anyone else if they come near me.'

'I'm afraid I shall have to lock you up, Joseph.'

'Take me and hang me if you like.'

Knowles showed him the knife Clarke Enderby had given him. 'That's it,' said Bones. 'That's the one I did it with. The big blade.'

The inquest on Eyre Petchell was opened on Saturday afternoon and after viewing the body and hearing the witnesses the jury retired for half an hour before bringing in a verdict of wilful murder. They added, however, the caveat that Bones had been subjected to great provocation, though not to an extent which would justify them charging him with the minor offence, presumably that of manslaughter. The funeral later took place at St Michael's church.

Joseph Bones never went to trial at Lincoln. Experts who examined him while he was in prison asserted that he was unlikely to understand what was going on during the trial, and the Lincoln Prison governor himself said, 'It is the most peculiar case I have ever known. Sometimes he understands what is said to him and at other times he appears to understand nothing. At times he is extremely violent and requires two or three warders to restrain him.'

It was thus pretty obvious that Bones' abrasiveness, unpredictability and violence were due to an underlying mental condition. At the time, however, he was judged to be of unsound mind and unfit to stand trial. He was ordered to be jailed indefinitely.

Nine

SHOTS IN THE NIGHT
William Clarke, 1877

Newark is a market town on the River Trent. It stands on the old Roman Fosse Way which connects Newark with Lincoln, and also, more recently, on the Great North Road, though the A1 now bypasses the town. From the earliest times its importance has been due to its being the centre of communications. In the time of Edward the Confessor the town belonged to the Earl of Mercia and his wife Lady Godiva, famous for riding naked through the town of Coventry to induce her husband to reduce the taxes for the poor. Later it was taken over by a succession of bishops of Lincoln, which is only sixteen miles away. Bishop Bloet built the castle, and it was rebuilt by Bishop Alexander, from 1123-33, and about this time the bridge over the Trent was constructed. The town became one of the most important centres for the wool and the cloth trade in the whole country. Kings visited the town and King John died there of dysentery in 1216. In the sixteenth century, King Henry VIII made his break with Rome and established the Church of England, with himself as head of the Church. But the vicar of Newark would not accept this, and was promptly executed on the orders of the king.

But the turbulent history of Newark really began during the civil war. The town became one of the centres for the Royalist cause, raised 600 soldiers and engaged in raids on other towns supporting the Parliamentary faction. Not surprisingly, the town came under siege from the Parliamentarians early in 1644, but was relieved later that year. Early the following year it was under siege again, and again rescued, but by the end of the year, when the third siege began, the Royalists had lost heavily at the battle of Naseby. Early the next year Charles I ordered the town to surrender and the castle was reduced to the ruin it largely is today.

In the Victorian era, the prosperity of the town increased. River traffic was of great importance, bringing in timber, grain and coal and taking out malt and flour. The Great North Road was the major route to London with seven stage coaches per day to and from the capital. Coaches also went to Lincoln and Nottingham. The town was an important place for brewing (the Empress of Russia was said to be fond of Newark beer), linen weaving, tanning, wood-turning and boat-building. More recently, the clothing industry has continued to prosper, together with the manufacture of agricultural machinery and the food industry.

People who were born or educated in the town include Sir Donald Wolfit, the Shakespearian actor, and Rupert Sheldrake, a biologist of international repute and the author of ten books. But in this story we will be concerned with four men who lived in Newark in 1877 and had far less illustrious reputations. The four men were William Clarke, forty-four, William Fletcher, twenty-seven, George Garner, thirty, and George Wood, who was also thirty. Clarke and Wood gave their occupations as 'brickmaker'. At the time there doesn't seem to have been any brickmaking in Newark, so it was quite likely that they were employed in Lincoln, which did have a substantial brickmaking industry at the time. The other two, Fletcher and Garner, were labourers. But all of them were part-time poachers. William Fletcher was well known to the local gamekeepers as an experienced poacher and had been in prison many times. But the older man, Clarke, was the more experienced criminal, who went under the aliases Western, Burk, Ross, Gray and John Willis, but was more commonly called 'Slenderman' by his associates. But little is known about the other two, Garner and Wood.

What is known is that they all met at William Fletcher's house in Newark on the evening of 29 January 1877. Garner and Wood arrived together, and when they reached the house they found Clarke already waiting there with Fletcher. Garner had brought his shotgun with him, and Fletcher had one of his own. For some time they discussed where to go poaching, eventually deciding to make for Eagle Wood. This was one of several which had been part of the estate of Eagle Hall. It was about halfway between Newark and Lincoln and about two or three miles north of the Fosse Way, near the village of Swinderby. In terms of distance it was about eight or nine miles from Newark and it would have taken about a couple of hours of brisk walking to get there. According to George Wood, they

Newark Market Place in the 1850s. (Courtesy of Nottingham Historical Film Unit and www.picturethe past.org.uk – NCCE 003931)

arrived at about ten o'clock at night. William Clarke was carrying one of the guns and Fletcher carried the other.

Normally the shooting season for pheasants is from the beginning of October to the beginning of February. At the end of the season, the gamekeeper normally pens the hen pheasants in with the cock pheasant and the resulting eggs are usually reared under chickens. When they hatch, the gamekeeper lives close to the young birds in a small hut near the rearing ground, since they are fed five or six times a day from feed cooked on the spot. He also has to keep an eye out for predators: foxes and stoats were caught by the use of gin traps, now thankfully made illegal, which were baited with rotting meat. After a few weeks the young pheasants are released into the woods, since pheasants are woodland birds, usually still penned and fed by the gamekeeper. Eventually they will be left to fend for themselves with only occasional feeding. But the gamekeeper or gamekeepers will still patrol the woods at night to discourage poachers.

When the four poachers reached Eagle Wood they searched for pheasants nesting in the trees, keeping as quiet as they could so as not to disturb the birds. They eventually found two birds. Clarke shot at one and brought it down and then, after a suitable interval, when the commotion which the gunshot had arisen in the birds had died down, Wood fired at the other and brought that down. After searching for some time, however, they found no more birds. Clarke then suggested that they split up. One of the guns belonged to Garner, though Clarke seemed to be using it, and he suggested that Garner and himself separate from the other two. The other gun belonged to Fletcher, so it seemed reasonable to leave that with him and Wood. This arrangement was agreed. Fletcher and Wood decided to stay in Eagle Wood and Clarke said he knew some good woods for game near Norton Disney. Fletcher and Wood said that they would meet the other two later in the night by the gate into the woods on the road to the village of Swinderby40

'Don't be a coward, George! Come on, I know where all the gamekeepers live. You'll be all right with me.'

Woods near Norton
Disney.

Garner reluctantly followed. When they reached the woods they found some birds almost immediately and Clarke shot them and gave them to Garner. 'You take them. There'll be plenty more for me later.'

But he was wrong. Possibly the birds had been disturbed by the shots and dispersed, but at all events they found no more. Garner again suggested going home, but Clarke, who perhaps felt that he would be going home empty-handed if they did, said, 'Let's try one last wood. There is another quite near here and it's loaded with birds.' So they moved on to another wood. But it was here that disaster struck.

They didn't know it, but the shots that Clarke had fired had been heard by three gamekeepers, Henry Walker, Charles Wells, and man named Lynn. They were employed by a Mr Graham, who rented the woods for raising pheasants for shooting. Lynn was despatched for assistance while the other two searched for the poachers. When they were close enough they could hear Clarke and Garner walking through the fallen leaves and the small broken branches which littered the ground beneath the trees. Wisely, the two poachers didn't speak much, but they were easily followed because they didn't realise that anyone had heard the shots. The gamekeepers followed them into the new wood. Suddenly Walker and Wells realised they were close to the poachers. They hid behind a substantial tree and saw two shadowy figures walking in a wide ride ten or twelve yards away. The light was not strong from the fitful moon, but because the men were walking in a relatively wide and open space they were seen. The watchers came out cautiously into the ride behind the poachers to follow them, but, quiet as they were, they were heard. Clarke and Garner turned and saw them.

The two poachers turned tail and ran. But Garner was hampered by the heavy sack of dead birds he was carrying and it was easy for the gamekeepers to keep up with them. Clarke, who was in front, turned to see his companion labouring behind him; the two keepers were keeping their distance, but clearly still behind them. Clarke raised his shotgun. 'If you come any closer, I shall shoot.'

Main Street,
Norton Disney.

But Walker was not put off. 'We're not armed. Put the gun down and fight like a man!'

But Clarke merely swore, turned and ran off again. The watchers followed, but they didn't want to get too close in case the poacher decided to use the gun. On the other hand, however, they didn't want to lose the couple should they decide to dash off into the tree cover – and, in fact, they did lose them for a while. But suddenly, Clarke popped up before them. They had obviously got too close without realising it. He raised the gun to his shoulder. 'I told you before. I'll shoot if you come too close.'

Walker raised his arms in a placating motion, but he still said, 'It's no use shooting or running. We've got men surrounding these woods – you can't get away.

For a moment Clarke seemed undecided. Should he take the chance of shooting and trying to get away in the melee which would follow, or should he give up the gun and surrender? In the end he decided to do neither. He put up the gun and dived off into the woods, Garner following as well as he could. For a while it seemed to the two poachers as if they had finally shaken off their pursuers. They came to a small stream which was crossed by a plank bridge and rushed across it. But perhaps the creaking of the loose plank as they pounded over it gave them away, for not far beyond that they came out into a wide glade in the woods and suddenly, behind them, the two gamekeepers appeared as if they had arisen out of the ground.

But this time, William Clarke had had enough. He turned to face them and went down on one knee. The shotgun was raised to his shoulder. The two gamekeepers, Walker in the lead, came to an abrupt halt. Perhaps they realised that they had at last come too close and that Clarke was now determined to fire. George Garner also realised this, for he shouted, 'Don't shoot. For God's sake, don't shoot!' But his words were drowned out by the discharge of the gun. Henry Walker screamed and went down, clutching his left leg. Clarke and Garner both disappeared into the darkness.

Back at the Eagle Woods, Fletcher and Wood had gone to the main gate of the wood which gave on to the Swinderby road to wait for Clarke and Garner to return. They lay on a bank at the side of the road for over an hour, but then gave up and went home.

Cobb Hall, Lincoln.

Henry Walker was taken on a horse and cart to Mr Graham's house and a doctor was called. Edward George Wake, described as a surgeon, came from Collingham, a couple of miles to the south west of Swinderby. He did what he could for the wounded gamekeeper, trying to remove as many shots as he could from the left knee. Walker, who had lost a lot of blood, was subsequently taken home and put to bed. He lingered for several days before dying of what the surgeon described as blood poisoning, no doubt due to the toxic nature of the lead shot. At the post-mortem, the surgeon found the marks of thirty-six pieces of lead shot which had entered the left leg, and ten more in the right leg.

When Henry Walker regained consciousness he was asked if he had recognised who had shot him, and he said he had – it was William Fletcher. This was confirmed by Charles Wells. Fletcher was visited by the police the next morning, and soon after that he, George Wood and George Garner were taken into custody. William Clarke had disappeared from his lodgings and could not be found. When the adjoined inquest into the death of Henry Walker was held on 19 February 1877 the jury brought in a verdict of guilty of wilful murder against all four men.

It is tenant of English law that if several persons are concerned in a criminal enterprise and during this someone is killed, even if only one person actually committed the murder, all the people concerned in the enterprise are deemed to be equally guilty. The hunt for William Clarke, which was conducted by Superintendent Brown of the Kesteven Police, went on. A £50 reward was posted for his capture and he was reported as having been seen in Grimsby, Hull and Yarmouth. All these leads were run down by the diligent police officer.

In the early part of February a man appeared at the White Horse public house in Lowestoft. He gave the name John Willis and told the licensee, Mrs Elizabeth Beel, that he had a shotgun for sale. She pointed him the direction of a local pawnbroker called Edward Lark and Willis dully pawned the gun there. He went back to the White Horse and, engaging the landlady in conversation, learned that she had a son who had a small fishing boat. Willis arranged to hire the boat and the son to take him to Ireland during the following week.

Executioner Marwood.

MARWOOD, his Cobbler's Shop and Trade Card.

WM. MARWOOD,

EXECUTIONER,

CHURCH LANE,

HORNCASTLE,

LINCOLNSHIRE, ENGLAND.

But while this was going on, information reached the ears of Supt Brown and he journeyed to Lowestoft on 15 February, took possession of the gun at the pawnbrokers and went to the White Horse. There he arrested Clarke, alias Willis, and brought him back.

When the Lincolnshire Spring Assizes opened on Monday, 5 March 1877 all four men went on trial for murder. But the prosecution offered no evidence against three of the men and only William Clarke was prosecuted for murder. It may seem strange that no evidence was offered against George Garner as he was plainly associated in the crime – and indeed, in law, would have been an accessory before the fact. But it was pretty obvious that because the identification of the shooter was in doubt – the two gamekeepers who saw the incident both identified Fletcher, though they afterwards changed their minds to Clarke – the prosecution did a deal with Garner. If he gave evidence against Clarke, the prosecution would offer no evidence against him. And this is what happened. Garner identified Clarke as the man who shot Walker, and William Clarke was convicted of murder. He was sentenced to be hanged, and on 26 March 1877 he was executed by William Marwood on the roof of Cobb Hall.

Ten

A KIND OF JUSTICE?
John Carrott, 1858

The figure of justice which stands on top of many court houses and public buildings is usually depicted as the Lady Justice. She follows the Roman goddess of justice Justitia or the Greek goddess Dike and carries a sword and scales. But in many statues she is blindfolded. This is supposed to depict that justice is meted out without fear or favour, but to many people justice is often thought to be blind – and never more so than the case of John Carrott.

In 1858, John Carrott lived in the village of Hogsthorpe, in those days quite a large village a mile or so from the village of Chapel St Leonards which is on the Lincolnshire coast. Hogsthorpe is some seven miles north of Skegness and six miles south east of Alford. Its name has nothing to do with pigs (although plenty of pigs were reared around the village), but derives from the Old Norse *Hogg's Thorpe*, which meant the village of a man called Hogg. The village had a water course to the south and east, called the Willoughby High Drain. It also had a substantial church, St Mary's, originally built in 1393, a Primitive Methodist chapel and also a Wesleyan Methodist chapel. There was a school, built in 1857, with a master's house; at one time it had seventy pupils. The village had all the usual Victorian trades associated with large villages: bakers and brewers, plumbers and painters, a saddler and a miller, wheelwrights and blacksmiths, butchers and bricklayers – and of course a pub, the Blue Bell Inn, usually referred to by the locals as the Bell.

John Carrott and his wife Eliza lived a little way out of the village in a very small cottage with only one room downstairs. He was twenty-five and she was a year of two older. They had a two-and-a-half-year-old son in October 1858. John was a farm worker and Eliza – who was described as short, but well built, with a lively personality – also helped out during harvest times and was thought to be nearly as strong as her husband when it came to heavy farm labouring. But it didn't seem to do her much good, for Carrott was a surly morose man, who often beat his wife.

On Thursday 23 October, they were in fields to the south of the village, owned by a farmer called John Mountain, helping to feed a thrashing machine operated by Edwin Vinter.

Hogsthorpe sign.

During a break in their labours she confided in Vinter that she had saved 7s from her wages and that her husband had his eye on this money, but she was not going to let him have it. The following morning, Friday, they started thrashing at about half past five on the farm of a William Graves. But John Carrott came without his wife.

'Is she badly?' asked Vinter.

'No she's not badly,' said Carrott, 'but I've given her the damndest thrashing she ever had in her life. And I hope she will be either dead or run away when I get home!'

Vinter raised his eyebrows but said nothing. But plainly Carrott had not finished. 'She also said she would have the police on me. So if you see him coming, you tell me. I'll give him a good run for his money. He won't catch me!'

Later that morning, between ten and eleven o'clock, Eliza called at the home of Charlotte Smith (who lived about 300 yards away from her). Eliza's lip was swollen and her face was extensively bruised.

Charlotte, who was surprised to see her, said, 'I thought you were supposed to be thrashing at Mr Graves' this morning?'

'I did go part of the way. But I just couldn't manage it. I had to come home.'

'Has he been beating you again?'

Eliza began to weep. This surprised Charlotte, for though she had seen the effects on her friend of Carrott's beatings before she had never seen her so distressed. She put her arms around Eliza and slowly the crying subsided. Between sniffs and sobs Eliza confessed that her husband had given her such a thrashing that morning as she had never had before. He had slammed her head against the wall several times and when she screamed in pain and terror he rushed to the front door and locked it, shouting: 'You beggar, I'll have you!' Then he had flung her to the floor and knelt on her, grasping her neck with one hand and her hair with the other and squeezing her throat until she lost consciousness. When she came to he had gone.

Charlotte shook her head as if in disbelief, although she knew full well that what Eliza had said was true. 'Why don't you leave him?' she asked.

Hogsthorpe High Street.

'I dare not!' Eliza croaked through her damaged throat. 'If I did and he ever met me afterwards he would murder me.'

Her words may seem melodramatic, but it would have been difficult for Eliza to move out of the village. Travel was not easy for poor people and even to get to a nearby village would mean a long walk; then she would find it difficult to support herself and her child, as women in those days usually had little money of their own. So even though the village she lived in was large, she would have found it difficult to keep out of Carrott's way if she left him.

Little is known about what went on the following day, but on Saturday evening a William Keal was walking home in the village when he overtook Eliza. He knew her and there was enough light for him to see that she had a couple of black eyes. 'You've been fighting again,' he joked.

Eliza tried a tremulous smile. 'We are unfortunately always at that.' She went on to tell him that her husband had given her a severe thrashing early on Friday morning. He had again knocked her down, got hold of her hair and tried to choke her. She had screamed: 'Jack, you're killing me!' And he shouted back in reply, 'I mean to do it! I'll knock the bloody row out of you!' He had banged her head several times against the wall. She stopped and rubbed the back of her head, uttering, 'Here the grievance lies', which presumably meant that she was still having pains in her head. William Keal left her by the bridge over the drain next to her own house and did not see her again.

According to John Carrott, Eliza fetched him later that same night from the Blue Bell in Hogsthorpe, but no witnesses were able to confirm his story. Mrs Jane Johnson was another neighbour of the Carrotts. It was the usual practice for Eliza to drop in to see her every Sunday morning. But on this particular Sunday, she did not come. Later that Sunday morning, Mrs Johnson saw John Carrott feedings his pigs. Then after that he went round

St Mary's church, Hogsthorpe.

picking up sticks as if he was going to make a fire. This was an occupation which usually occupied Eliza, but on this particular morning there was sign of her. Later that day he was seen in some stubble fields belonging to a Mr West, with a gun. This was not unusual as this was the beginnings of the pheasant- and grouse-shooting season and Carrott could well have been acting as a beater for his more wealthy neighbours. Or he could merely have been shooting rabbits.

The next sighting of John Carrott came the next day, Monday, when he was working in the fields of a Mr Graves of Chapel St Leonards. Graves had a friend staying with him, a John Panton, who lived in Horncastle. They were out together in the fields which bordered the seashore, being separated from it by a high sea bank. Panton noticed Carrott continually climbing the bank. He would go to the top and then look inland. From there you could see the village of Hogsthorpe. Afterwards he noticed Carrott sitting on a wheelbarrow with his head in his hands. He and Graves asked Carrott if he was feeling unwell, but the man denied it and went on with his work.

Later that day, at about five o'clock, another neighbour of the Carrotts, William Harriman, called at their house. He was there to make arrangement for the next day's work. He knocked on the door, but got no reply. But he thought that he could hear the sound of a child crying. Soon after this another neighbour, Mrs Johnson, came by. Harriman asked her if she knew where Mrs Carrott was. She said she didn't, but both listened at the door and Mrs Johnson thought she heard the child calling, 'Mummy!' She shouted to the child through the stout door and the child answered, but she couldn't make out what the child said.

'There's something wrong here,' said Mrs Johnson. There was a pane of glass missing from a window near the door and Mrs Johnson managed to squeeze her way in. She pounded

Bridge over
Willoughby
High Drain,
Hogsthorpe.

her way up the stairs and almost immediately came rushing downstairs, screaming, 'She's dead!'

Mrs Johnson unlocked the front door and Harriman himself also climbed the stairs. But the sight that met his eyes horrified him. The young boy was naked and standing near his mother, who was on the bed in the bedroom. Eliza was lying on her back; she was dressed in her nightdress, but it was open to the waist and there was a shotgun lying across her legs. She was obviously dead: the body was cold, the smell overpowering. Mrs Johnson found a shirt for the little boy to put on and her screams soon attracted other neighbours.

A local farmer, Robert Addison, had been passing when he heard the noise, and he came to investigate. He too went up the stairs and saw the body of Eliza Carrott. He thought that she had been dead for a considerable time. He had been on his way to Richard West's house and he went on and found a local doctor there, Mr W.B. Rainey. He told them about the death at the Carrott house and they all went back there. Dr Rainey observed that the room bore evidence of a severe struggle. The bedclothes were torn and twisted and Mrs Carrott was on her back with one leg drawn up and her fist clenched. Her lips were swollen. There were bruises on her neck and throat, her breast and her left hand and arm. He considered that she must have received very brutal treatment, and that this looked very much like a death caused by violence. Mr West sent for the police and PC Ransome was soon on the scene. He too took in the disordered bedroom, the bruising on the body and the gun lying across the legs, and he went in search of John Carrott. He found him eventually at eleven o'clock that night, asleep at his father's house in the village. He roused him and told him that he was being apprehended on a charge of murdering his wife, who had been found in bed under very peculiar circumstances.

Carrott muttered, 'Very well. I must go, I suppose. I can't help; it's a very bad job.'

The inquest was held the next day. As was usual, the jury were taken to view the body in the house where the death had taken place. But such was the decomposition of the body that it had to be taken out in the open air for identification and inspection. The inquest

Sea bank at Chapel St Leonards.

was adjourned until the following Thursday to allow the post-mortem to take place; this was undertaken by Mr Rainey and Mr Johnson, both doctors living in the village. They carried out the examination on the kitchen table. When the inquest was resumed and witnesses were heard, the jury returned a verdict of wilful murder against John Carrott and he was committed for trial at the Lincoln Assizes.

The Lent Assizes began on Saturday, 12 March 1859. When the Lord Chief Justice Campbell and the Honourable Justice Erle arrived at Lincoln they were met at the Midland station by the High Sheriff of the County, his chaplain, the County under Sheriff and his deputy, the City Sheriff and the City under Sheriff – and of course the usual contingent of trumpeters and javelin men, all in their imposing livery. The judges were conveyed in carriages while the whole procession proceeded up the High Street, which was lined with spectators. At the bottom of Lindum Hill, the Lord Chief Justice disembarked and was conducted to the Sessions House, which used to stand there. Mr Justice Erle was conveyed in his carriage up the hill to the judge's lodgings which stood, and still stands, near the eastern entrance to the castle.

On Tuesday morning, at 9 o'clock, Mr Justice Erle took his seat at the head of the crown court in the castle grounds and opened the case against John Carrott, who was charged with the murder of his wife, Eliza. He was defended by Mr Macaulay, whilst the prosecution was in the hands of Mr Adams. When it came to the medical evidence, however, the chief doctor who carried out the post-mortem, Mr Rainey, was not in court and the judge criticised him strongly for this, saying that the reason for his absence was trivial. However, they had to reply on the evidence of Mr Johnson, who had assisted in the examination. Having described the external bruising that the body had sustained, Johnson pointed out that the scalp showed no external wound. Underneath, however, several bruises were detected – showing evidence of severe blows – but the skull was not fractured. The brain was in a highly congested state, much in the same condition as would occur from suffocation (either through hanging, drowning or strangulation).

Judges' lodgings, Lincoln.

Loose blood was discovered in the skull, evidence of the rupture of a blood vessel in the brain, and in the left hemisphere a large clot of blood was found which was sufficient to cause death very quickly.

But the defence argued that the weakening of the blood vessels could have been caused by the beating Carrott gave his wife on Friday (he admitted assaulting his wife on that day), or that it could have been caused by a fall. She was seen alive and apparently well on Saturday night, so she must have died between then and the following Monday. In that time, any little excitement might have triggered the actual rupturing of the blood vessels and her subsequent death. Although Carrott's beating was a contributory cause of his wife's death, it did not amount to murder. The jury agreed with him, and he was found guilty only of manslaughter which did not carry the death penalty. John Carrott thus escaped the hangman, but the judge imposed the harshest sentence he could, life imprisonment. So was justice blind in this case or not?

Eleven

BORSTAL BOY

Kenneth Strickson, 1948

The idea of a youth prison was first discussed in 1895 by the Gladstone Committee, the object being to separate youths from older prisoners in adult prisons. The system was first established in 1902 with an institution called Borstal Prison in the village of Borstal, near Rochester in Kent. But the idea subsequently spread to all parts of the UK. Over the years, the name has come to be used for all types of youth institutions including Approved Schools and Detention Centres.

The Borstal Institutions were run by the prison service. The original idea was to reform seriously delinquent young people from ages sixteen to twenty-one, but in the 1930s the age was raised to twenty-three. The institutions were designed to provide regular work, discipline and also education, but the main emphasis was on discipline. The court sentence was called 'Borstal Training' and was often two to three years in length. And many young offenders much preferred a normal prison sentence because it was considerably shorter. All the Borstal inmates were forced to wear short trousers. This, in the early years, was perhaps not too much of an imposition, but over the years, as long trousers became more the garb of youths and young men, it became a demeaning rule. Short haircuts were also the order of the day, and in an era when longer hair became more fashionable this was also a trial to many boys.

The only form of corporal punishment used in Borstals was the birch, and it has been said that this was only used for attacks on staff or mutiny. Allegedly it was rarely used. Caning was common in Approved Schools, which were institutions for younger youths; any absconders were usually caned when they were caught and returned to the establishment. Approved Schools, which were created in 1933, were split into three groups: Junior, Intermediate and Senior. They were modelled on ordinary boarding schools, but many were known for strict discipline.

The different Borstals catered for different types of offender. Feltham Borstal, for example, was usually for boys of sixteen to eighteen years who were fairly easily handled. Camp Hill Borstal on the Isle of Wight, on the other hand, took boys of the same age range but who were more difficult and hardened types. Lowdham Grange had sixteen to twenty-one year olds who responded well to training and would be fit for early release. Sherwood Borstal was housed in the old Bagthorpe Prison in Nottingham. It catered for older boys, twenty to twenty-three, often who had been let out on licence from other institutions but had reoffended and been recalled. It was tough regime. One ex-Borstal boy has claimed that 'more often than not, Borstals were breeding grounds for bullies and psychopaths'.

Mrs Irene May Phillips was one of two matrons at the Sherwood Borstal. She was forty-six years old, a kindly, mothering type of woman who was very popular with all the young men. In November 1948 she had been at the Borstal for just a year. One of her charges was twenty-one-year-old Kenneth Strickson, who had been there since June the year before. One of his jobs was to clean the chapel and to assist Matron Phillips whenever she was in the vestry. On Thursday 18 November, Strickson confided to one Enoch Roberts that he had made a suggestive remark to Mrs Phillips about her breasts, but she had taken it in good part and merely remarked that it was a good thing that she was broadminded.

It was obvious that he had taken her reaction as a sign that she might look favourably on him. He did not realise, or chose to ignore, the fact that she had not reprimanded him or reported him because she had treated his remark as frivolous and coming from someone who was hardly more than a youth. And she hadn't complained because she did not want to get him into trouble. He appeared excited and said to Roberts, 'I am going to try and see what I can get out of her later.'

But the other inmate was appalled. 'Don't be a fool,' he said. 'You'll get three years for that.' But Strickson would not be persuaded. He was convinced that his charms would overpower any resistance she might put up. And in any case, he did not expect her to put up any resistance.

'Don't be crazy,' said Roberts. 'She might shout out or scream for help. What are you going to do then?'

'She won't,' replied Strickson confidently. 'But if she does I shall just have to cosh her.'

It was about eleven o'clock the next morning when Harry Bradshaw, another inmate, wanted to get in touch with Mrs Phillips. He knocked on the door of her office, but heard nothing. Assuming that she had gone to the vestry, he went in search of her; however, that door too was closed and locked. Then he looked down and saw something seeping out from underneath the door. It looked very much like blood.

While this was going on, Kenneth Strickson was standing by the front gate. The door was open and a building party was working outside. Strickson approached the prison officer guarding the gate. 'I've had permission to go and help the building party outside.'

The gatekeeper looked him up and down. 'Where's your pass?'

'I must have left it on my bed.'

'Well you'll have to go and get it then, won't you? You don't go out of the gate without a pass.'

Strickson turned away. He would have to go and see the chief officer to get a pass, who would then ask him what he wanted the pass for. As he walked along he turned over in his mind: what excuse could he offer? He could think of nothing that would get him out of the gates and away to freedom, and he realised that they would soon find out what he had done. When he finally knocked on the door of the chief officer's room and was asked

Interior of the courthouse, Nottingham Assizes, in the Shire Hall. (Courtesy of Nottingham Historical Film Unit and www.picturethepast.org.uk – NTGMO 15348)

to enter, he marched up to Christopher Morrow's desk. 'Will you go to the chapel, sir?' he croaked. 'I've killed the matron.'

Morrow looked at Kenneth Strickson in astonishment. But he was a man of action and few words. He got up and scooped up the keys for the chapel. Then he called for a prison officer to take charge of Strickson while he made his way to the chapel. The sight which met his eyes when he opened the door of the vestry was one he would remember all his life. It was like a slaughter house: there was blood over the walls and the splintered remains of what afterwards turned out to be two smashed chairs. In the middle of all the destruction lay Irene Phillips, covered in blood and with fearful injuries to her head. Incredibly enough, she was still breathing. Morrow called for an ambulance and the police, and Mrs Phillips was rushed to hospital.

Detective Inspector Corbett said afterwards: 'something of appalling savagery had taken place and someone had gone completely berserk in that vestry.' And when he interviewed Strickson later, the young man said, 'I don't know what made me do it.' He was charged with causing the matron grievous bodily harm and taken by the police to Lincoln Prison. Although doctors worked desperately to save her life, Mrs Phillips died later that afternoon. The charge against Strickson was now murder.

Kenneth Strickson went on trial at the Nottingham Assizes in the Shire Hall on Wednesday, 1 December 1948, before Mr Justice Lynskey. The prosecution was in the hands

Lincoln Prison.

of Mr E. Clayton and he was defended by Mr R. T. Paget. Professor J. M. Webster, Director of the Home Office Forensic laboratory at Birmingham, reported that Mrs Phillips had suffered extensive bruising to her body and to her face. She had cuts to the back of her head and had a fractured skull and spine. In his opinion, most of the wounds had been sustained while she was on the ground. He could find no evidence of a sexual attack.

Mr Paget had a difficult task in defending Strickson, who refused to say what had happened in the vestry that morning. The defence counsel attacked Enoch Roberts, in cross examination, when the inmate gave evidence of the conversation he said he had had with Strickson. Mr Paget brought up Roberts's past criminal record, a series of break-ins and a rape, and accused him of making up the story to get his discharge earlier. But the sheer ferocity of Strickson's assault on the matron weighed heavily against him. Mr Paget pleaded insanity for his client at the time of the attack, saying the Strickson's father had been an inmate of an asylum and had died from swallowing a fork. Strickson had come from a broken home. His mother had taken no interest in him and he had been in Approved Schools since an early age.

At that time the test of insanity was still governed by the McNaghten Rules which stated that for a 'not guilty through insanity verdict' the defendant must be shown that he did not know the nature and quality of his act, or if he did know he didn't know that it was wrong. The prosecution pointed out that Strickson had signalled his intention of attacking the matron if necessary by his conversation with Roberts; he had reported what he'd done to the chief officer soon after the attack, clearly showing that he recognised the enormity of his crime. The jury agreed and reached a guilty verdict in just twenty-two minutes. Strickson was sentenced to death. A petition was soon raised for mercy because of his youth, but this rejected by the Home Secretary on 21 March. On the following day, he was hanged in Lincoln Prison by Albert Pierrepoint.

Twelve

A MURDEROUS PAIR

Henry Carey and William Picket, 1859

'Will you come with me and rob the old man?'

'What, old Stephenson?'

'Yes. I've heard that he's been to market today to sell some pigs, so he's bound to have a lot of money in his pockets.'

The two young men, Henry Carey (who was twenty-four) and William Picket (twenty), were standing outside the Ship Inn at Sibsey. And the man they were talking about, William Stephenson, was sixty-four years old and lived at Northlands, a small hamlet a mile or so north of Sibsey. It was a Wednesday evening in March 1859.

'But he knows you,' said Picket. 'You used to live with him, didn't you?'

Carey shifted his feet. 'Well he took me in once when I was thrown out of my own home,' he said grudgingly. 'But he's a miser and a miserable old so-and-so besides. And if we cover our faces with pocket handkerchiefs he won't know it's us.'

Picket nodded his head in agreement. 'Yes, I think I've got a couple in my pocket. One I pinched from my girlfriend,' he giggled.

Northlands village
sign.

'Here's the plan,' said Carey, in an important-sounding voice. 'We'll go back in the pub and say that we are going to spend the night in your father's boat. You know what old Richardson's like [Richardson was the keeper of the pub]. He'll soon be telling us we've had enough to drink and to clear off home. So we go out before old Stephenson does and cut ourselves a couple of canes from the hedge, just in case we're attacked by dogs out on the fens.' Here he gave Picket a broad wink and the young man giggled again. 'Then we lie in wait for the old man. Rob him when he turns up and we're away before he realises what's happened or who it is.' Picket nodded in agreement and the two young rogues went back into the Ship Inn.

In the 1850s, Sibsey was a substantial village with a population of over a 1,000 and some 200 houses. It was five miles to the north of Boston, which in those days was the largest town in Lincolnshire, and some twenty-seven miles from Lincoln. Sibsey had a station on the East Lincolnshire Railway, a Wesleyan chapel, a substantial church, St Margaret's, and three pubs. A fuller account of the village and its history appears in *Murder and Crime: Boston*. Northlands (or, to give it its earlier name, Norlands) on the other hand was a much smaller village, but it had a Primitive Methodist chapel and a free school which had been established in 1846. It was also further out on the Fens. Previously, the Fens around Boston had been dank areas largely covered by water with people living on small islands in the water waste. Draining of the Fens took place from about 1630 onwards, and the result was many small waterways which eventually emptied into the River Witham. The waterway near Northlands is today called the Stone Bridge Drain and a road through the village leads to a stone bridge. After drainage, land became available for cultivation and was divided up into the rectangular fields which we now see. Enclosures around Northlands were completed by 1813.

Sibsey village with the church in the background.

Methodist chapel, Northlands.

Early on Thursday morning, 17 March 1859, a young woman called Mary Sempter, a neighbour of William Stephenson, came out of her little cottage in Northlands and saw what she thought was a piece of cloth floating in a deep ditch nearby. She got a stick and poked at the cloth and found that it was the shirt on a man and as she poked, the body rolled over in the water and she saw that it was William Stephenson. She rushed immediately to the old man's cottage and rang for his son, who lived with him; he came out and confirmed that the body was indeed that of his father. With the help of two other neighbours he was able to get his father out of the ditch, but there was nothing they could do for the old man. He was quite dead. The local police were called and they made an examination of the place where the old man had been found in the water.

There was abundant evidence of a struggle having taken place. The grass was flattened down and there were bloodstains on the grass. There were also signs that something had been dragged along the grass field from a nearby road and a hedge had been flattened by the side of the waterway as if something had been pushed through it or over it. There were also footmarks on the road. In those days the roads in the Fens were often covered with a layer of silt to compact and solidify the small stones underneath. But the roads became soft in wet weather and easily showed footmarks. Bloodstains were found on the road and it was obvious that the attack must have started nearby. In addition, several pieces of wood were found covered in blood and hair, which had obviously been used as clubs.

That same morning the two young men, Carey and Picket, had been woken by a farmer called Sands when he went into his barn and fell over Picket's legs. They had not slept in Picket's father's boat, as they had given out, but had gone to Sands' barn. They soon took themselves off to the Ship Inn. Later that day, William Stephenson's son also went to the public house. He noticed the two young men there and it looked to him as if they had dried blood on their clothes. Without saying anything to them he left and went for the police. Later that day, Carey and Picket were taken into custody by the police. They were searched at the police station – and on Carey they found a knife, which was afterwards identified by Stephenson's son as having belonged to his father. They were interviewed by the police, and Picket made the following statement:

The Old Schoolhouse, Northlands.

Myself and Carey left the public house at between 10 and 11 o'clock and went towards the house of my father. But he had gone to bed and we could not get in. At Carey's request we crossed the drain in my father's boat to go to Sands place to get some rabbits he had shot and said we could have. As we went Carey took a large stake from the hedge and told me to do the same. He said we might be attacked by dogs. But I wouldn't take one. When we had gone a little way we overtook Stephenson. Carey said, 'Let's kill the old b——, I think he's got some money.' I advised him not to but he went up to the old gentleman and hit him on the head with his stake. He put his hand in the man's pocket and took out some money. He again hit him with the stick. He told me to take hold of the old man's head and I refused. Then he said he would serve me the same if I did not do it. I then helped him throw the old man into the ditch. But the old man got to his feet in the ditch and tried to climb out the other side. I rushed round to help him, but Carey came as well and continued to beat him with his stake until it broke and he threw it in the ditch. He told me that the old man was dead as he didn't stir in the water at all. Then he showed me that he had taken one sovereign from him, a half a crown, some papers and two bags. We went to the field gate of one of my father's fields and buried the papers under some turf there. Then we went to Sand's barn. The next morning we went to the Ship and on the way Carey gave me the sovereign and took the knife for himself. I hid my sovereign in the thatch at Richardson's furnace house. Carey took out the bags he had taken from Stephenson, put a stone in them and threw them in Richardson's pit.

The pair were taken before the magistrates and, in view of Picket's confession, Captain Bicknell, chairman of the magistrates, ordered the pit in Richardson's yard to be dragged; the thatch of the furnace house was also searched, and the bags and the stolen money were retrieved. But what Picket had not realised was that confessing to being there at the perpetration of the crime, and participating even to a small extent in it, made him liable to being accused of murder. And both were sent for trial on that charge.

Northlands Bridge.

The trial opened at the summer assizes in Lincoln on 28 July 1859 before Mr Justice Williams. Mr Stephens and Mr Huish appeared for the prosecution, and William Picket was defended by Mr Flowers. Henry Carey was not represented by counsel, since his family could not afford to pay for one. In those days there was no system whereby counsel could be appointed and be paid by the court as there is today. Picket pleaded not guilty and Carey, when asked to plead, replied in a loud firm voice, 'I am guilty of the robbery but not of the murder.'

The prosecution had a strong case. Blood was found on the prisoners' clothes and boots. The footmarks found on the road clearly showed that the attack had begun there and the impressions matched the boots of the two young men. In anticipation of Picket's defence, the prosecution pointed out that the assault was plainly the work of two men and the murder could not have been committed by one man alone.

Although Carey was not represented, he made a statement in court. He said that he had promised Picket that he wouldn't say a word about the affair unless he was forced to, but now that Picket had accused him he was bound to tell the truth. It was Picket who had first broached the idea of robbing the old man. He himself had not been keen, but Picket said that if he didn't come with him he would go alone. Picket produced the pocket handkerchiefs and said he would hold the old man's head while Carey went through his pockets. Carey struck the man twice on the arm and once on the head and it was Picket who flung the man into the ditch. Plainly, they were blaming each other for the affair, and the truth was probably very far from what they said.

Picket's counsel tried to get the jury to agree that the verdict on Picket should not be 'guilty of murder' but only of being an accomplice after the fact. But the judge pointed out that they had both admitted being present at the scene of the murder and that the violence of one became, in point of law, the violence of the other. If the jury believed the evidence which had been put before them they were bound to find them both guilty. And so it turned out.

Stone Bridge Drain.

The jury returned after only half an hour with verdicts of guilty against both men. The judge, in tremulous tones, pronounced the sentence of death.

Before their executions they both made confessions which were probably a lot nearer the truth than their previous ones. They confirmed that they had decided to rob William Stephenson, and had therefore left the pub before he did to lay in wait for him by the side of the road. When he came up he saw them and said, 'Hullo my lads, who are you? Why don't you lay in one of these barns rather than by the side of the road?' They then wrestled him to the ground and Picket held him while Carey went through his pockets. But neither of them had realised the resistance that the old man would put up, and they had to resort to violence to subdue him, culminating in beating him to death. They both expressed remorse for their awful deed.

They suffered the extreme penalty of the law on Friday, 5 August 1859, being executed on the top of Cobb Hall at the corner of Lincoln Castle before a crowd of about 12-13,000. The hangman was Thomas Askern from York. The execution turned out to be the last public hanging at Lincoln.

Thirteen

NO PROVOCATION
Leonard Holmes, 1945

The village of Walesby in Nottinghamshire is some sixteen miles to the north west of Newark and about twenty miles west of Lincoln. It is famous for its forest, probably part of the original Sherwood Forest of Robin Hood fame. In the 1940s there lived in the village one Leonard Holmes, who had been a lorry driver before the war, and his wife Peggy Agnes and six children. In 1945 Leonard was thirty-two and Peggy thirty. They lived in a bungalow in Central Avenue, as its name suggests near the shops in the village, and only a short walk from the pub on the main road, the Carpenters Arms. Leonard Holmes had joined the Army and in 1943 he had been stationed at Huddersfield. There he met a Mrs May Shaw and they began a relationship.

He kept the relationship secret from his wife and continued to come home at intervals as if nothing was amiss. But this was not very satisfactory for Mrs Shaw. She kept on at him to regularise their relationship; to get a divorce from Peggy and marry her. But Holmes put her off by saying that it was unwise of him to make the change while he was still in the forces, since he might be posted abroad at any minute. But once he was demobilised he would do something about it, and Mrs Shaw had to be satisfied with that.

Leonard Holmes was demobilised at the end of October 1945 and not long after this, in fact on Sunday 18 November, his parents, who lived nearby, came to visit. They spent the day with the family and their grandchildren and then in the evening, after the children had been put to bed, they walked down with Leonard and Peggy to the Carpenters Arms. They had a convivial evening. There were a few servicemen in the bar, mostly RAF personnel from the nearby RAF stations, and men like Leonard from the village who had been demobilised. The group walked back to the bungalow and Leonard's parents said goodbye and left.

But all was not well with Holmes. Before he and Peggy went to bed, he began an argument with her. He afterwards claimed that he accused her of flirting with two airmen who had been standing at the bar, saying that she had been exchanging 'nods and winks' with them. She denied this, but after further argument, again according to Holmes, she admitted adultery, saying, 'If it will ease your mind I have been untrue to you. I know I have done wrong, but I have no proof that you haven't done the same with Mrs Shaw!'

This admission apparently stunned Holmes. He had not realised that Peggy knew anything about Mrs Shaw and it also came as a shock for him to realise that Peggy could be unfaithful too. The embarrassment of being found out, coupled with the knowledge that he too had been cuckolded, drove him to anger. He picked up a coal hammer from the fireplace and hit her once on the side of the head with it. She collapsed on the floor, but, as she wasn't yet dead, he climbed on top of her and strangled her with his bare hands. It was about two o'clock in the morning. He spent the rest of the night cleaning up the bloodstains on the floor, then took Peggy's body upstairs to their bedroom and put her on the bed.

The next day was Monday. He made breakfast for the children and saw them off to school. He told them that their mother was not well and had stayed in bed and that they should go to their grandparents' house after school and stay there until he contacted them. Then he caught a train for Huddersfield. He had previously sent a telegram to Mrs Shaw to meet him at the station and this she duly did. He said that Peggy had left him and would not be coming back, and that he was now free to be with Mrs Shaw.

Central Avenue,
Walesby.

But Leonard Holmes had made a serious mistake. He had left the body of his wife in the bungalow. Later that Monday, his brother paid an unexpected visit to the house and discovered the body. He immediately got in touch with the police. Leonard was the obvious suspect, and when he came back on the Tuesday the police were waiting for him when he got off the train at Retford station. He was arrested, and the next morning charged with the murder of his wife.

His statement contained the words, 'Yes, it happened on Sunday night. It was over something she said. I hit her with a hammer. There is only one answer to the charge. I admit it.'

He was brought to trial on a charge of murdering his wife. The trial took place at the Nottingham Assizes, held in the Shire Hall, Nottingham on 28 February 1946, before Mr Justice Charles. His defence was one of provocation – which, if believed, would have reduced the charge to one of manslaughter, still a serious charge but one that did not carry the death penalty. He claimed that that his attack on his wife was not premeditated, as would have to have been the case if it was murder, but was brought on by a fit of anger when his wife confessed to adultery. He had hit her with the hammer in the heat of the moment, not intending to kill her, and then had placed his hands around her neck to keep her quiet.

But the argument was refuted in part by the evidence of prosecution witness Professor Webster, Director of the West Midlands Forensic Laboratory. In his opinion, Peggy Holmes would have survived the hammer blow to the head. It was the squeezing of the throat which killed her. In other words, Holmes had strangled her. This, the prosecution pointed out, could hardly be a domestic argument which got out of hand. If he really did not set out to kill her, surely he would have stopped after the hammer blow.

But the clincher was a telegram which Holmes had sent to Mrs Shaw on the Saturday, the day before the murder. It said, 'See you on Sunday or Monday for sure. Be prepared. OK. All fixed. Len.' It seemed fairly obvious that when he sent the telegram he knew something was about to happen, that he would be free to marry Mrs Shaw after Sunday or Monday.

Carpenters Arms, Walesby.

Retford station.

And thus the attack on Peggy on Sunday night or early Monday morning was more likely to be a planned one, a premeditated act. Holmes' answer to this was that he had seen a packed suitcase of Peggy's and realised that she was about to leave him; this, he claimed, was the reason for the telegram. It was a feasible argument, but no evidence was brought forward to show that Peggy had in fact packed any such suitcase or had been preparing to leave him.

The judge ruled that, on the evidence presented to them, it was not open for the jury to bring in a verdict of manslaughter on the grounds of provocation; the jury therefore took his advice and brought in a verdict of murder. Leonard Holmes was then sentenced to death. But because this was an important point of law, the case went to the Court of Appeal on 25 March. The court upheld the verdict of the lower court, but the argument went on and was carried right up to the House of Lords. The law lords there then made a definitive, ruling that: 'Words (in this case a confession of adultery) could not be of sufficient provocation to reduce a murder charge to manslaughter'.

It was only after this, on 28 May, that Leonard Holmes went to the scaffold. The hangman was said to be Thomas Pierrepoint – but, according to the autobiography of Albert Pierrepoint, who succeeded his uncle as official chief hangman, Thomas retired in 1943, so there seems some doubt as to who actually hanged Leonard Holmes.

BIBLIOGRAPHY

BOOKS

Browne, Douglas G., *Sir Travers Humphries*, George G. Harrap, 1960

Eddleston, John J., *The Encyclopaedia of Executions*, John Blake, 2002

Fairlie, Gerard, *The Reluctant Cop*, Hodder and Stoughton, 1958

Gagen, N.V., *Hanged at Lincoln (1716-1961)*, Private Publication

Gray, Adrian, *Crime and Criminals in Victorian Lincolnshire*, Paul Watkins, 1993

Gray, Adrian, *Lincolnshire Headlines*, Countryside Books, 1993

Gray, Adrian, *Lincolnshire Tales of Mystery and Murder*, Countryside Books, 2004

Gray, Adrian, *Tales of Old Lincolnshire*, Countryside Books, 2005

Hill, Sir Francis, *A Short History of Lincoln*, Lincoln Civic Trust, 1979

Halliwell, J.O., *A Narrative of the Bloudy Murders*, Private Circulation, 1860

Harrison, Richard, *Criminal Calendar*, Jarrolds, 1951

Humphreys, Sir Travers, *A Book of Trials*, William Heinemann, 1953

Ketteringham, John, *Lincolnshire People*, The King's England, 1995

Knowles, Leonard, *Court of Drama*, John Long, 1966

La Bern, Arthur, *Haigh – The Mind of a Murderer*, W.H. Allen, 1973

Lane, Brian and Gregg, Wilfred, *The New Encyclopaedia of Serial Killers*, Headline, 1996

Lincolnshire Villages, Lincolnshire Federation of Women's Institutes, 2002

Mee, Arthur, *Lincolnshire*, Hodder and Stoughton, 1949

Moorland, Nigel, *Hangman's Clutch*, Werner Laurie, 1954

Robinson, David N., *The Book of Louth*, Barracuda Books, 1979

Simpson, Professor Keith, *Forty Years of Murder*, Harrap, 1978

Stockman, Rocky, *The Hangman's Diary*, Headline, 1993

Turton, Kevin, *Foul Deeds and Suspicious Deaths in Nottingham*, Wharncliffe Books, 2003

Vale, David, *Lincoln – A Place in Time*, Friends of Lincoln Archaeological Research and Excavation, 1997

Wade, Stephen, *Lincolnshire Murders*, Sutton Publishing, 2006

Wade, Stephen, *Hanged at Lincoln*, The History Press, 2009

Webb, Duncan, *Crime Is My Business*, Frederick Muller, 1953

Wilson, Patrick, *Murderess*, Michael Joseph, 1971

NEWSPAPERS

Boston Gazette and Lincolnshire Commercial Advertiser
Boston Guardian and Lincolnshire Independent
Boston, Lincoln, Louth and Spalding Herald
Grimsby Evening Telegraph
Horncastle News
Lincoln Rutland and Stamford Mercury
Lincolnshire, Boston and Spalding Free Press and South Holland Advertiser
Lincolnshire Chronicle
Lincolnshire Echo
Lincolnshire Gazette
Lincolnshire Times
Louth and North Lincolnshire Advertiser
Louth Standard
Louth Times and Mablethorpe and Sutton Advertiser
Nottingham Evening Post

MAGAZINES

Lincolnshire Life
Murder Casebook, Vol. I, Part 6, John George Haigh, Marshal Cavendish, 1990
Murder in Mind, Issue 16, John George Haigh, Marshal Cavendish, 1997
Real Life Crimes, Vol. I, Part 14, John Haigh, Eaglemoss Publications, 1993